All-in-One English Listening:

Interactions for Listening & Speaking, Reading & Writing

PUBLISHED BY THE HAKMUN PUBLISHING, CO.

1F Seorabol B/D, 198 Naeja-dong, Jongno-gu, Seoul, 110-053, Korea
TEL: (02) 738-5118 FAX: (02) 733-8998

Publisher: Kim, Joo-yeon
Writers: Charles Langdon / Yong-Jin Shin
Editorial Assistant: Lee, Soo-kyoung
Cover Design: Park, Hyung-bin
Illustration: I&D
CD Recording: YEA SUNG RECORD'S CO.

First published 2011

Price: ₩13,800(CD included)

ISBN 978-89-467-9130-5 (93740)

◀ 각과 지도 요령 ▶

Warm-up: Pre-listening Exercises 단계

A와 B는 대화 내용을 학생들에게 두 번씩 들려준다. 교재 여백에 내용을 메모할 수 있다.

Background for Listening Practice 단계

A는 원문을 듣도록 한다. 원문을 playback시켜 한 번 더 들려줄 수 있다.

B는 단어 풀이를 참고로 문장의 빈칸을 채울 수 있도록 학생들에게 시간적 여유를 준다. 학생들이 빈칸을 다 채웠다면 instructor는 확인하기 위해 학생들에게 질문을 한다.

C는 다시 원문을 듣도록 한다.

Oral Practice & Writing Exercises 단계

A는 원어민이 읽는 문장을 듣고 학생들에게 따라 하게 한다. instructor는 문장을 듣고 학생들이 반복할 수 있도록 녹음기 작동을 잠시 멈춘다. 문장마다 학생들이 따라 읽도록 한다. 또다른 방법으로는 1번~5번까지 전부 들려준 후 한 문장씩 읽도록 할 수도 있다.

B는 내용에 따라 빈칸에 쓰도록 시간적 여유를 준다.

C는 원문을 들으면서 빈칸을 채우도록 한다.

D는 원어민이 원문을 다시 한 번 읽을 때 확인하고 정답을 수정하도록 한다.

Model Dialogue 단계

A는 대화의 내용을 학생들이 듣도록 한다.

B는 대화 내용을 반복하여 따라 하도록 한다.

C는 대화 내용을 다시 한 번 들려주며 빈칸에 단어를 채우도록 한다.

D는 C번의 내용을 다시 들으면서 정답을 수정하도록 한다.

Pair Work: Interactions 단계

학생 두 명을 A, B로 나눈 다음 대화 내용을 연습하게 한다. 다 끝나면 역할을 바꾸어 연습하도록 시간을 준다.

Listening Comprehension Check-up 단계

본문 내용을 들은 다음 질문내용에 따라 답을 쓰도록 한다.

답을 쓸 수 있는 시간적 여유를 준다. 이어서 본문 내용을 20자 이내로 요약할 수 있는 시간적 여유를 다시 준다.

Listening Test 단계

test 1은 종합적으로 회화 내용에 따라 해당 그림에 번호를 쓰도록 하고, test 2는 대화 내용을 다시 한 번 들려주며 지시문에 따라 대답을 하도록 한다.

Listening Comprehension Exercises 단계

두 사람의 대화 속에서 맞는 내용에 따라 해당번호를 고르도록 한다.

※ 1시간의 수업 동안 각 unit을 전체적으로 반복하여 들려줄 수 있다.

Table of Contents | 차례

Preface

Traditionally, listening & speaking skills were emphasized for Korean students to learn English in the classroom and practice English in the language laboratory. Numerous hours were spent for them to improve their English proficiency. And many language laboratories were installed to develop students' proficiency of English in many middle and high schools, and even in colleges and universities.

Today, listening and reading skills are initially focused on the principles of 'Comprehension precedes production.' These two kinds of integrative skills are necessary for learning English. But these suggestions won't be accomplished easily. First, English itself is not socialized in Korea. Second, when listening skills are focused on first, students can not understand the content or meaning of listening, for they don't have enough prior knowledge to understand listening exercises. In this case, hearing, not listening, is developed.

Reading skills can provide students the prior knowledge necessary to practice or comprehend listening. To supplement reading skills, a writing skills will be provided at the same time. Namely, reading and writing should be taught integratively and simultaneously. Reading sections help students to understand contents. Difficult words, in advance, can be presented in the key word section. To help students comprehend the meaning of the words some exercises are provided.

| 머리말

전통적으로 우리나라에서는 학교에서 영어를 공부할 때 듣기와 말하기가 강조되어 왔고 그래서 어학실습실에서 영어 훈련을 했습니다. 많은 시간을 이 능력을 키우는 데 쏟아부었습니다. 그리고 학생들의 영어 실력을 향상시키기 위해 많은 중·고등학교에 어학실습실이 만들어졌고 이런 현상은 대학들도 마찬가지였습니다.

오늘날 듣기와 읽기 능력은 원래 "Comprehension precedes production." (먼저 이해를 해야 말하고 쓸 줄 안다) 원칙에 초점이 맞춰져 있습니다. 듣기와 읽기의 이 두 가지 능력은 영어를 배우는 데 꼭 필요합니다. 그러나 이 능력은 쉽게 길러지지 않습니다. 첫째로 영어 자체가 우리 사회에서 그렇게 널리 통용되지 않기 때문입니다. 둘째로 우리 사회에서 영어가 널리 통용되고 있지 않아 듣기 능력이 떨어진다는 첫 번째 사실에만 초점이 맞춰지면 학생들은 듣는 것의 내용이나 그 의미를 이해할 수 없습니다. 듣기 연습을 이해하는 데 필요한 사전지식이 충분하지 않기 때문입니다. 이럴 경우 단순히 듣는 능력(hearing)은 늘지만 청취력(listening)은 향상되지 않습니다.

읽기 능력은 학생들에게 듣기 훈련을 하거나 내용을 이해하는 데 필요한 사전지식을 제공해줍니다. 읽기 능력을 보완하기 위해 쓰기 능력이 동시에 제공될 것입니다. 다시 말하면 읽기와 쓰기는 통합적으로 그리고 동시에 배워야 하는 것입니다. 읽기 섹션은 학생들이 내용을 이해하는 데 도움을 줍니다. 그에 앞서 어려운 단어들이 키워드 섹션에 제시됩니다. 단어의 의미를 이해하는 데 도움을 주기 위해 연습문제를 마련해 두었습니다.

To the Teachers

All-in-One English Listening: Interactions for Listening & Speaking, Reading & Writing is the integration of listening, speaking, reading and writing. The listening and speaking practice course is one of the developments of English language proficiency. The listening and reading course is also one of the developments of English language proficiency. This priority is appropriate in the learning theories and principles of learning and teaching.

The most important thing is that students should learn and understand English language. To activate the listening skills, students need prior knowledge. Beginning learners of English never understand contents when they just listen to the tape. So, in advance, teachers have to teach contents using visual materials. Basically, reading should be taught with writing practice. Integrations of reading and writing can make students facilitate listening capability better.

Learners have their own learning styles. Particularly, most Korean students prefer visual learning styles. Students' visual learning styles should be satisfied in the process of learning and teaching. The use of visual materials in the process of teaching reading and writing will make students understand contents of listening and speaking.

This English language laboratory textbook initially focuses on background for listening practice. Students can comprehend dialogue or conversation on the basis of student's prior knowledge after learning reading and writing. As a result, background knowledge will help students in listening and will give them a willingness to learn English.

This book consists of 22 units, each with a different, interesting thematic focus. Each unit will cover two hours. Students can learn English dialogue without teachers' help.

| 선생님들께

*All-in-One English Listening: Interactions for Listening & Speaking, Reading & Writing*은 듣기, 말하기, 읽기 그리고 쓰기를 통합적으로 다룬 책입니다. 듣기와 말하기 훈련 과정은 영어 실력을 늘리는 데 필요한 과정의 하나입니다. 듣기와 읽기 훈련 과정 또한 마찬가지입니다. 이같은 중요성은 학습이론들과 학습 교수의 원리들에서도 강조되는 것입니다.

가장 중요한 것은 학생들이 영어라는 언어에 대해 알고 이해해야 한다는 것입니다. 듣기 능력을 향상시키기 위해서는 사전지식이 필요합니다. 영어 테이프를 들려주기만 해서는 영어를 처음 배우는 사람들은 그 내용을 전혀 이해하지 못합니다. 그러므로 선생님들은 미리 그 내용을 시청각 교재로 보여줘야 합니다. 또한 기본적으로 읽기는 쓰기와 함께 가르쳐야 합니다. 읽기와 쓰기를 함께 가르치면 학생들의 듣기 능력이 훨씬 더 향상됩니다.

학생들은 배울 때 각자 나름대로 스타일이 있습니다. 우리나라 학생들은 특히 시청각 교재를 통한 학습을 좋아합니다. 시청각 교육은 배우고 가르치는 과정에서 학생들에게 만족을 주어야 합니다. 읽기와 쓰기를 가르치는 과정에서 시청각 교재를 사용하면 학생들은 듣기와 말하기의 내용을 훨씬 잘 이해할 수 있습니다.

이 교재는 원래 듣기 훈련을 위한 기초지식에 초점을 맞춰 만들어졌습니다. 학생들은 읽기와 쓰기에서 익힌 사전지식을 바탕으로 대화나 회화의 내용을 이해할 수 있습니다. 결과적으로 배경지식은 듣기 훈련에 도움을 주고 아울러 학생들에게 영어를 배우고 싶다는 즐거운 마음을 갖게 해줄 것입니다.

이 교재는 22단원으로 구성되어 있으며 각 단원마다 서로 다르면서도 재미있는 주제들을 다루고 있습니다. 한 단원을 공부하는 데 2시간 정도 걸릴 것입니다. 선생님의 도움 없이도 학생들이 영어 대화를 배울 수 있도록 꾸몄습니다.

Structure of the Unit

Warm-up: Pre-listening Exercises

- There are two mini-dialogues.
- These are relevant to the title.
- Students practice listening considering the title.
- Students can take a note or dictate two dialogues in the margin.

Background for Listening Practice

- Have students read the passage while listening to the tape.
- The reading passage is relevant to the title and pre-listening exercises.
- This section focuses on reading comprehension.
- To help students comprehend the passage some words are translated in English.
- Have students fill some words in the appropriate slot. This is writing exercise.
- Have them select some words in the passage and write them. This is also writing exercise.
- Lastly, the passage is given for them to understand and memorize.

Oral Practice & Writing Exercises

- Five sentences are chosen in the passage for students to keep retain.
- Have students listen to the passage without looking at the whole passage.
- Students write answers in the blank.
- Have students give a dictation to understand the passage completely.

Model Dialogue

- The short but meaningful dialogue is written, focused on a passage students can read and understand.
- Have students repeat the dialogue for oral practice and pair work.
- Model dialogue is given for students to give a dictation for memorization.

Pair Work

- Have students practice speaking with his/her partner two times.
- They can practice model dialogue without looking at the dialogue.

Listening Comprehension Check-up

- Students read, repeat and dictate the reading passage through the various steps.
- Again, have them listen to the passage to answer the questions correctly.
- Finally, have students summarize the passage in less than twenty words.

Listening Test & Listening Comprehension Exercises

- This is to test students' own listening capacity.

단원의 구성

Warm-up: Pre-listening Exercises
- 두 개의 짧은 대화가 나옵니다.
- 이 대화들은 제목과 관련 있는 내용입니다.
- 학생들은 제목을 염두에 두고 듣기 훈련을 합니다.
- 학생들은 책 여백에 메모를 하거나 두 개의 대화 내용을 받아쓸 수 있습니다.

Background for Listening Practice
- 학생들에게 테이프를 들으며 조용히 지시문을 따라 읽게 합니다.
- 지시문은 제목과 pre-listening exercises의 내용과 관련이 있습니다.
- 이 섹션은 읽고 이해하기에 초점이 맞춰져 있습니다.
- 학생들이 지시문의 내용을 이해하는 것을 돕기 위해 단어 중 몇 개를 골라 영어 뜻풀이를 붙여놓았습니다.
- 학생들에게 빈칸을 알맞은 단어로 채우게 합니다. 이것은 쓰기 훈련입니다.
- 학생들에게 지시문에서 단어를 몇 개 뽑아 써보게 합니다. 이것도 쓰기 훈련입니다.
- 마지막으로 학생들에게 문장을 이해하고 외우게 합니다.

Oral Practice & Writing Exercises
- 학생들이 계속 잊어버리지 않도록 지시문에서 뽑은 문장 다섯 개가 제시됩니다.
- 학생들에게 지시문을 보지 않고 듣도록 지시문을 들려줍니다.
- 학생들은 정답을 빈칸에 적어 넣습니다.
- 학생들이 지시문을 완벽하게 이해할 수 있도록 받아쓰기를 시킵니다.

Model Dialogue
- 학생들이 지시문을 읽고 이해하는 데 초점이 맞춰진, 짧으면서도 내용이 함축적인 대화가 제시됩니다.
- 회화 훈련과 짝활동 학습을 할 수 있도록 학생들에게 대화를 반복시킵니다.
- Model Dialogue는 학생들이 받아쓰기를 해 대화를 외울 수 있도록 하기 위한 것입니다.

Pair Work
- 학생들에게 자기 짝과 말하기 연습을 두 번씩 하게 합니다.
- Model Dialogue 대화를 보지 않고 외워서 할 수 있게 합니다.

Listening Comprehension Check-up
- 여러 단계를 거치면서 학생들은 지시문을 읽고, 반복하고, 받아쓰게 됩니다.
- 다시 지시문을 들려주고 질문에 정확히 대답하게 합니다.
- 마지막으로 학생들에게 지시문의 내용을 20단어 정도로 요약하게 합니다.

Listening Test & Listening Comprehension Exercises
- 이것은 학생 개개인의 듣기 능력을 테스트하기 위한 것입니다.

Unit 1 Postcards

Warm-up: Pre-listening Exercises

Listen to the mini-dialogues two times each looking at the pictures below. You can write or make notes of the mini-dialogues in the margin.

A. It's a postcard.

B. This postcard is very beautiful.

Background for Listening Practice

***A.* Read the following paragraph with a low voice while listening to the tape.**

Postcards always spoil my holidays. Last summer, I went to Italy. I visited museums and sat in public gardens. A friendly waiter taught me a few words of Italian. Then he lent me a book. I read a few lines, but I did not understand a word. Every day I thought about postcards. My holidays passed quickly, but I did not send any cards to my friends. On the last day I made a big decision. I got up early and bought thirty-seven cards. I spent the whole day in my room, but I did not write a single card!

***B.* Study the following words and then fill in the blanks with the correct words.**

postcard	a card on to which the sender must affix a stamp
holiday	a day on which one is exempt from work
museum	a place where objects are exhibited
decision	a determination arrived at after determination
bought	past of verb 'buy'; to acquire possession
spent	past of verb 'spend'; to use up or pay out

1. I'm going to give a beautiful ________ for my girlfriend.
2. At last I made a big ________ .
3. On the way home I ________ a piece of tasteful bread for my child.
4. I visited Korea and saw a ________ .
5. He ________ some money for his unhealthy grandmother.
6. What are you going to do on ________ ?

***C.* Listen to the tape again.**

Oral Practice & Writing Exercises

***A.* Now let's practice. Please repeat, considering the paragraph in the "Background for Listening Practice".**

1. Postcards always spoil my holidays.
2. I visited museums and sat in public gardens.
3. Every day I thought about postcards.
4. On the last day I made a big decision.
5. I spent the whole day in my room.

***B.* Change the present verb into the past verb.**

1. spoil ➡	____	2. lend ➡	____
3. understand ➡	____	4. pass ➡	____
5. buy ➡	____	6. write ➡	____

***C.* Now dictate the following sentences while listening to them once.**

Postcards always spoil my holidays. Last summer, I ____ to Italy. I ____ museums and sat ____ public gardens. A ____ waiter taught me ____ few words of ____. Then he lent ____ a book. I ____ a few lines, ____ I did not ____ a word. Every ____ I thought about ____. My holidays passed ____, but I did not ____ any cards to my friends. On the ____ I made a ____ decision. I got ____ early and bought cards. I spent ____ whole day in ____ room, but ____ did not write ____ single card!

***D.* Listen again and check the answers.**

Model Dialogue

A. ***Listen to the dialogue.***

A: John took a trip to California by car.

B: That's a long trip. How long did it take him?

A: About six weeks. He wanted to see as much as possible.

B: What route did he take?

A: He went to California by the southern route.

B: When did he cross the Mississippi?

A: He crossed it the first time at New Orleans.

B. ***Repeat the dialogue above.***

C. ***Now dictate the following sentences while listening to them once.***

1. John took a trip to ________ by car.
2. What ________ did he take?
3. He went to California by the ________ route.
4. When did he ________ the Mississippi?
5. He ________ it the first time ________ New Orleans.

D. ***Listen again and check the answers.***

Pair Work: Interactions

Practice the following dialogue with your partner. Student 1 takes part A and student 2 takes part B. Then switch.

***A*:** John took a trip to California by car.

***B*:** That'a long trip. How long did it take him?

***A*:** About six weeks. He wanted to see as much a possible.

***B*:** What root did he take?

***A*:** He went to California by the southern route.

***B*:** Where did he cross the Mississippi?

***A*:** He crossed it the first the at New Orleans.

Listening Comprhension Check-up

Listen to the paragraph again and write your answers in the space provided below. The instructor asks each question two times.

1. Where did he spend his holidays last summer?

2. Who taught him a few Italian words?

3. Did he send some cards to his friends?

4. How many cards did he buy on the last day?

5. Did he write cards for his friends?

Can you summarize the paragraph 'Postcards' above in less than twenty words?

LISTENING TEST

Test 1

Listen to the conversation 1~3 and write the number of each conversation on the correct picture.

Test 2

Listen to the conversations again and fill in the correct information.

1. a) The address of the store is ______________.
b) The name of the store is ______________.

2. a) The telephone number is ______________.
b) The woman's area code is ______________.

3. a) The girl's last name is ______________.
b) Her social security number is ______________.

LISTENING COMPREHENSION EXERCISES

Choose the best answer to each question.

1. (A) The coffee is much better this morning.
(B) The coffee tastes extremely good.
(C) The coffee isn't very good.
(D) This morning he definitely wants some coffee.

2. (A) The two classes meet in an hour and a half.
(B) The class meets three hours per week.
(C) Each half of the class is an hour long.
(D) Two times a week the class meets for an hour.

3. (A) A few minutes ago, the flight departed.
(B) The flight will start in a while.
(C) They are frightened about the departure.
(D) The plane is going to take off soon.

4. (A) He hasn't yet begun his project.
(B) He's supposed to do his science project next week.
(C) He needs to start working on changing the due date.
(D) He's been working steadily on his science project.

5. (A) At the post office.
(B) In a florist shop.
(C) In a restaurant.
(D) In a hospital delivery room.

Unit 2 Education in Korea

Warm-up: Pre-listening Exercises

Listen to the mini-dialogues two times each looking at the pictures below. You can write or make notes of the mini-dialogues in the margin.

A. Korean children start by the age of seven or eight.

B. How many years do children attend?

Background for Listening Practice

A. ***Read the following paragraph with a low voice while listening to the tape.***

Elementary education is compulsory and free for every child in Korea. Most children start school by the age of seven or eight. They attend six years of elementary school, three years of middle school, and three years of high school. The money for the public schools comes from taxes, and the central government is responsible for the educational system. It establishes Education Boards in each province which guide and inspect each school. Children are required to attend through elementary school.

B. ***Study the following words and then fill in the blanks with the correct words.***

compulsory	obligatory, mandatory, enforced
attend	to be present at, go to
government	the organization or agency through which a political unit exercises authority and performs functions
responsible	liable to be called on to answer
establish	bring into existence
province	an administrative district or division of a country
inspect	to examine officially, look over

1. Is elementary education ______ and free for every child in Korea?
2. How many years do college students ______ ?
3. The central ______ will be responsible for the educational system.
4. Education Board in each province ______ each school.
5. When is the elementary school going to be ______ ?
6. Human beings should be ______ for their behavior.
7. There are eight ______ in Korea.

C. ***Listen to the tape again.***

Oral Practice & Writing Exercises

A.* *Now let's practice. Please repeat, considering the paragraph in the "Background for Listening Practice".

1. Elementary education is compulsory for every Korean child.
2. Most children start school by the age of seven or eight.
3. The central government is responsible for the educational system.
4. The central government establishes Educational Boards.
5. Educational Boards inspect each school.

B.* *Change the adjective into the noun.

1. compulsory ➡ ________
2. central ➡ ________
3. responsible ➡ ________
4. educational ➡ ________
5. provincial ➡ ________

C.* *Now dictate the following sentences while listening to them once.

Elementary education is compulsory and free every ________ in Korea. Most ________ start school by ________ age of six. ________ Attend six years ________ elementary school, three ________ of middle school, ________ three years of ________ school. The money for ________ public schools comes ________ taxes, and the central government is responsible ________ the educational system. ________ establishes Education Boards ________ each province which guide inspect each school. ________ are required to ________ through elementary school.

D.* *Listen again and check the answers.

Model Dialogue

A. ***Listen to the dialogue.***

A**:** Did you pass the entrance exam?

B**:** Yes, but my score wasn't as high as yours.

A**:** Don't worry about that. The important thing is to pass.

B**:** Passing is important, but getting a high score is important, too.

A**:** Why? You don't need a scholarship, do you?

B**:** It would help if I could get one.

A**:** That's right. You've got three brothers and sisters in school, too.

B**:** Yes, all the way from elementary school to high school.

A**:** That must be very expensive for your father.

B. ***Repeat the dialogue above.***

C. ***Now dictate the following sentences while listening to them once.***

1. Did you pass the ________ exam?
2. Passing is ________, but getting a high ________ is important, too.
3. Why? You don't ________ a scholarship, do you?
4. ________ got three brothers and ________ in school, too.
5. That must be very ________ for your father.

D. ***Listen again and check the answers.***

Pair Work: Interactions

Practice the following dialogue with your partner. Student 1 takes part A and student 2 takes part B. Then switch.

***A*:** Did you pass the entrance exam?

***B*:** Yes, but my score wasn't as high as yours.

***A*:** Don't worry about that. The important thing is to pass.

***B*:** Passing is important, but getting a high score is important, too.

***A*:** Why? You don't need a scholarship, do you?

***B*:** It would help if I could get one.

***A*:** That's right. You've got three brothers and sisters in school, too.

***B*:** Yes, all the way from elementary school to high school.

***A*:** That must be very expensive for your father.

Listening Comprhension Check-up

Listen to the paragraph again and write your answers in the space provided below. The instructor asks each question two times.

1. Who is responsible for the educational system?

2. What does the central government establish?

3. What do Education Boards do?

4. When do Korean children start?

5. Are children required to attend through elementary school?

Can you summarize the paragraph 'Education in Korea' above in less than twenty words?

LISTENING TEST

Test 1

Listen to the conversations 1~4 and write the number of each conversation on the correct picture.

Test 2

Listen again and write the key words next to each picture.

LISTENING COMPREHENSION EXERCISES

Choose the best answer to each question.

1. (A) The professor drowned the cells in a lab.
(B) The lecture was long and boring.
(C) The professor divided the lecture into parts.
(D) The biologist tried to sell the results of the experiment.

2. (A) She needs to get a driver's license.
(B) Two pieces of identification are necessary.
(C) The man should check to see if he needs credit.
(D) A credit card can be used to get a driver's license.

3. (A) Housing within his budget is hard to locate.
(B) It's hard to find his house in New York.
(C) He can't afford to move his house to New York.
(D) Housing in New York is unavailable.

4. (A) The boss was working on the reports.
(B) He would have to finish the reports before the end of next month.
(C) He was directed to stay late and finish some work.
(D) He could finish the reports at home.

5. (A) The boisterous students made the teacher mad.
(B) The teacher angered the students with the exam results.
(C) The students were angry that the teacher was around.
(D) The angered students complained to the teacher.

Unit 3 Education in America

Warm-up: Pre-listening Exercises

Listen to the mini-dialogues two times each looking at the pictures below. You can write or make notes of the mini-dialogues in the margin.

A. We are going to school by the age of seven or eight in Korea.

B. How many years do the junior high school students attend?

Background for Listening Practice

A. ***Read the following paragraph with a low voice while listening to the tape.***

Education is compulsory and free for every child in the United States. Most children start school by the age of six. Some children attend eight years of elementary school and four years of high school. Others attend a six-year elementary school, a three-year junior high school, and a three-year high school. The money for free public schools comes from taxes, and each state is responsible for its own educational system. State legislatures set the educational requirements but leave the management of the schools in the hands of the local communities. Most states require their children to go to school until a certain age.

B. ***Study the following words and then fill in the blanks with the correct words.***

compulsory	obligatory, enforced
attend	to be present at
tax	a charge of money imposed by authority on persons or property for public purposes
legislature	an organized body having the authority to make laws for a political unit
requirement	something wanted or needed
community	a unified body of individuals, a body of persons or nations having a common history or common, social, economic and political interests

1. The ______ of a particular state or country is the group of people who have the power to make and pass laws.
2. Variations of this program can be arranged to suit your ______.
3. If you ______ an institution such as a school, or church, you go there regularly.
4. If something is ______, you must do it or accept it.
5. ______ is an amount of money that you have to pay to the government so that it can pay for public services.
6. The police haven't really done anything for the black ______ in particular.

C. ***Listen to the tape again.***

Oral Practice & Writing Exercises

A. Now let's practice. Please repeat, considering the paragraph in the "Background for Listening Practice".

1. Education is free for every child in the United States.
2. Some children attend eight years of elementary school.
3. Others attend a three-year junior high school.
4. The money for free public schools comes from taxes.
5. State legislatures set the educational requirements.

B. Write five nouns and five verbs which you heard in the paragraph.

	Nouns		Verbs
1.		1.	
2.		2.	
3.		3.	
4.		4.	
5.		5.	

C. Now dictate the following sentences while listening to them once.

Education is compulsory and free for every child in the United States. Most children start _____ by the age _____ six. Some children _____ eight years of elementary _____ and four years _____ high school. Others _____ a six-year elementary _____, a three-year junior _____ school, and three-year _____ school. The money _____ free public schools _____ from taxes, and _____ state is responsible _____ its own educational _____. State legislatures set _____ educational requirements but _____ the management of _____ schools in the _____ of the local _____. Most states require _____ children to go _____ school until _____ certain age.

D. Listen again and check the answers.

Model Dialogue

***A.* Listen to the dialogue.**

***A*: Hey, Billy. What classes are you going to take next semester?

***B*: I'm enrolled in chemistry, advanced composition, and political science.

***A*: Wow! That sounds like a tough schedule.

***B*: Yeah, my parents want me to go to Harvard University so I don't have a choice. What about you, Paul?

***A*: I'm going to take drama, ceramics, basic math, and physical education.

***B*: Man! I wish I had your schedule. It sounds like fun.

***A*: Yeah, I really like drama. Since my parents don't push me to go to college, I take the classes I want to take.

***B.* Repeat the dialogue above.**

***C.* Now dictate the following sentences while listening to them once.**

1. I'm enrolled in chemistry, _______ composition, advanced German and _______ science.
2. Yeah, my parents _______ me to go to Harvard University _______ I don't have a _______. What about you, Paul?
3. I'm going to _______ drama, ceramics, basic _______ and physical _______.
4. Man! _______________.
5. Yeah, I really like _______. Since my parents don't _______ me to go _______ college, I take the _______ I want to take.

***D.* Listen again and check the answers.**

Pair Work: Interactions

Practice the following dialogue with your partner. Student 1 takes part A and student 2 takes part B. Then switch.

***A*:** Hey, Billy. What classes are you going to take next semester?

***B*:** I'm enrolled in chemistry, advanced composition, and political science.

***A*:** Wow! That sounds like a tough schedule.

***B*:** Yeah, my parents want me to go to Harvard University so I don't have a choice. What about you, Paul?

***A*:** I'm going to take drama, ceramics, basic math, and physical education.

***B*:** Man! I wish I had your schedule. It sounds like fun.

***A*:** Yeah, I really like drama. Since my parents don't push me to go to college, I take the classes I want to take.

Listening Comprhension Check-up

Listen to the paragraph again and write your answers in the space provided below. The instructor asks each question two times.

1. Isn't Education in America free for every child?

2. How long do some children attend elementary school?

3. How can the money for free public schools be received?

4. Who is responsible for the American educational system?

5. Don't most states require their children to go to school?

Can you summarize the paragraph 'Education in America' above in less than twenty words?

LISTENING TEST

Test 1

Listen to the conversations 1~6 and write the number of each conversation on the correct picture.

Test 2

Listen again and write the key words next to each picture.

LISTENING COMPREHENSION EXERCISES

Choose the best answer to each question.

1. (A) Not all the bills have been paid.
(B) They don't have enough credit to pay the bills.
(C) What she said on the phone was not credible.
(D) He used a credit card to pay some of the bills.

2. (A) She'll call back quickly.
(B) She'll definitely be back by 4:00.
(C) She'll give it back by 4:00.
(D) She'll try to return fast.

3. (A) She hasn't seen Tim.
(B) Tim was there only for a moment.
(C) Tim was around a short time ago.
(D) Tim will return in a minute.

4. (A) She doesn't like the place he chose.
(B) She doesn't want to get into the car.
(C) She's glad the spot is reserved.
(D) They can't park the car there.

5. (A) There's plenty to eat.
(B) The refrigerator's broken.
(C) The food isn't in the refrigerator.
(D) He's not sure if there's enough.

Unit 4 An Exciting Trip

Warm-up: Pre-listening Exercises

Listen to the mini-dialogues two times each looking at the pictures below. You can write or make notes of the mini-dialogues in the margin.

A. Have you ever been to Australia?

B. I' d like to visit a famous temple in KyungJu.

Background for Listening Practice

A. Read the following paragraph with a low voice while listening to the tape.

I have just received a letter from my brother, Tim. He is in Australia. He has been there for six months. Tim is an engineer. He is working for a big firm and he has already visited a great number of places in Australia. He has just bought an Australian car and has gone to Alice Springs, a small town in the centre of Australia. He will soon visit Darwin. From there, he will fly to Perth. My brother has never been abroad before, so he is finding this trip very exciting.

B. Study the following words and then fill in the blanks with the correct words.

receive	getting something from others
engineer	a person who uses scientific knowledge to design, construct, and maintain engines and machines
firm	an organization which sells or produces something
centre	a middle part or point
Darwin	a city and important port in North Australia

1. We went to a party at the leisure ______.
2. ______ founded a theory of evolution.
3. Recently, most students want to be an ______.
4. The ______'s employees were expecting large bonuses.
5. They will ______ their awards at a ceremony in Stockholm.

C. Listen to the tape again.

Oral Practice & Writing Exercises

***A.* Now let's practice. Please repeat, considering the paragraph in the "Background for Listening Practice".**

1. I have just received a letter from my brother.
2. Tim is in Australia.
3. He has been there for six months.
4. He has just bought an Australian car.
5. My brother has never been abroad before.

***B.* Write five nouns and five verbs which you heard in the paragraph.**

Nouns	Verbs
1. ________	1. ________
2. ________	2. ________
3. ________	3. ________
4. ________	4. ________
5. ________	5. ________

***C.* Now dictate the following sentences while listening to them once.**

I have just received a letter from my brother, Tim. He is in Australia. He has been there for six months. Tim is an engineer. He is working for ________ big firm and he ________ already visited a great ________ of places in Australia. ________ has just bought an ________ car and has gone ________ Alice Springs, a small ________ in the centre of ________. He will soon visit ________. From there, he will ________ to Perth. My brother ________ never been abroad before, ________ he is finding this ________ very exciting.

***D.* Listen again and check the answers.**

Model Dialogue

A. *Listen to the dialogue.*

A: Wow! Australia is such a big country.

B: It sure is. How long have we been driving today?

A: About eight hours.

B: Eight hours? That's amazing. We have only passed through three towns all day.

A: I know. It's so different from Korea, isn't it?

B: Yeah. How often can you see kangaroos hopping along the highway?

A: Look! There's one now.

B: Let's stop and take a photo. Do you think it will smile for me?

B. *Repeat the dialogue above.*

C. *Now dictate the following sentences while listening to them once.*

1. It sure is. How ______ have we been driving today?
2. We have ______ through three towns all day.
3. It's ______ from Korea, isn't it?
4. How ______ can you see kangaroos ______ along the highway?
5. Do you think it will ______ ?

D. *Listen again and check the answers.*

Pair Work: Interactions

Practice the following dialogue with your partner. Student 1 takes part A and student 2 takes part B. Then switch.

***A*:** Wow! Australia is such a big country.

***B*:** It sure is. How long have we been driving today?

***A*:** About eight hours.

***B*:** Eight hours? That's amazing. We have only passed through three towns all day.

***A*:** I know. It's so different from Korea, isn't it?

***B*:** Yeah. How often can you see kangaroos hopping along the highway?

***A*:** Look! There's one now.

***B*:** Let's stop and take a photo. Do you think it will smile for me?

Listening Comprhension Check-up

Listen to the paragraph again and write your answers in the space provided below. The instructor asks each question two times.

1. What has the writer just received from his brother, Tim?

2. Is Tim an engineer or a doctor?

3. How long has he been in Australia?

4. Has he already visited many places or not?

5. Has Tim ever been abroad before or not?

Can you summarize the paragraph 'An Exciting Trip' above in less than twenty words?

LISTENING TEST

Test 1

Listen to the conversations 1~4 and write the number of each conversation on the correct picture.

Test 2

Listen again and write the key words next to each picture.

LISTENING COMPREHENSION EXERCISES

Choose the best answer to each question.

1. (A) He is leaving now.
(B) He has to go out of his way.
(C) He will not be leaving soon.
(D) He will do it his own way.

2. (A) He locked the door.
(B) He tried unsuccessfully to get into the house.
(C) He was able to open the door.
(D) He left the house without locking the door.

3. (A) She doesn't like to listen to turkeys.
(B) She thinks the dinner sounds special.
(C) She especially likes the roast turkey.
(D) She'd prefer a different dinner.

4. (A) He'll be busy with her homework tonight.
(B) He can't help her tonight.
(C) He's sorry he can't ever help her.
(D) He'll help her with her physics.

5. (A) Her eyes hurt.
(B) She thought the lecture was great.
(C) The class was boring.
(D) She didn't want to watch Professor Martin.

Unit 5 Fishing

Warm-up: Pre-listening Exercises

Listen to the mini-dialogues two times each looking at the pictures below. You can write or make notes of the mini-dialogues in the margin.

A. Fishing is my favorite sport.

B. How many fish did you catch?

Background for Listening Practice

A. Read the following paragraph with a low voice while listening to the tape.

Fishing is my favorite sport. I often fish for hours without catching anything. But this does not worry me. Some fishermen are unlucky. Instead of catching fish, they catch old boots and rubbish. I am even less lucky. I never catch anything-- not even old boots.

After having spent whole mornings on the river, I always go home with an empty bag. "You must give up fishing" my friends say, "It's waste of time." But they don't realize one important thing. I'm not really interested in fishing. I am only interested in sitting in a boat and doing nothing at all.

B. Study the following words and then fill in the blanks with the correct words.

favorite	markedly popular, constituting a favorite
catch	to capture, seize after pursuit
boots	a covering of leather or rubber for the foot and ankle, usually heavier and thicker than a shoe
rubbish	useless waste or rejected matter
waste	loss through breaking down of bodily tissue

1. Where is your ______ place?
2. What are you doing now, John? It is a ______ of time.
3. I tried to ______ many fish, but I got only a pair of ______.
4. ______ can be a cause of environment pollution.

C. Listen to the tape again.

Oral Practice & Writing Exercises

***A.* Now let's practice. Please repeat, considering the paragraph in the "Background for Listening Practice".**

1. Fishing is my favorite sport.
2. Some fishermen are unlucky.
3. I have spent whole mornings on the river.
4. I always go home with an empty bag.
5. They don't realize one important thing.

***B.* Write five nouns and five verbs which you heard in the paragraph.**

	Nouns		Verbs
1.		1.	
2.		2.	
3.		3.	
4.		4.	
5.		5.	

***C.* Now dictate the following sentences while listening to them once.**

Fishing is my favorite sport. I often fish for hours without catching anything. But this does not worry me. Some fishermen are unlucky. Instead _____ catching fish, they catch _____ boots and rubbish. I _____ even less lucky. I _____ catch anything--not even old _____.

After having spent whole _____ on the river, I _____ go home with an _____ bag. "You must give _____ fishing" my friends say, "_____ waste of time." But _____ don't realize one important _____. I'm not really interested _____ fishing. I am only _____ in sitting in a _____ and doing nothing at _____.

***D.* Listen again and check the answers.**

Model Dialogue

A. Listen to the dialogue.

***A*:** What did you do last Saturday, John?

***B*:** I went fishing with my friends.

***A*:** How many fish did your friends catch?

***B*:** All they caught was a pair of old boots and some rubbish.

***A*:** How about you?

***B*:** I was even less lucky. I didn't catch anything.

***A*:** Why did you go fishing then?

***B*:** I just like sitting in a boat and doing nothing.

B. Repeat the dialogue above.

C. Now dictate the following sentences while listening to them once.

1. What did you do ________, John?
2. I went ________ with my friends.
3. How ________ fish did your friends ________?
4. ________. I didn't ________ anything.
5. I ________ like sitting in a ________ and doing nothing.

D. Listen again and check the answers.

Pair Work: Interactions

Practice the following dialogue with your partner. Student 1 takes part A and student 2 takes part B. Then switch.

***A*:** What did you do last Saturday, John?
***B*:** I went fishing with my friends.
***A*:** How many fish did your friends catch?
***B*:** All they caught was a pair of old boots and some rubbish.
***A*:** How about you?
***B*:** I was even less lucky. I didn't catch anything.
***A*:** Why did you go fishing then?
***B*:** I just like sitting in a boat and doing nothing.

Listening Comprhension Check-up

Listen to the paragraph again and write your answers in the space provided below. The instructor asks each question two times.

1. What is the speaker's favorite sport?

2. What do some fishermen catch instead of catching fish?

3. How does the speaker spend his whole mornings?

4. What do his friends say when he goes home with an empty bag?

Can you summarize the paragraph 'Fishing' above in less than twenty words?

LISTENING TEST

Test 1

Listen to each sentence 1~10 and write the number of the sentence above any picture(occupation) that it matches.

Example : **1.** He always works indoors.

VOCABULARY

- always
- indoors
- uniform
- usually
- customers
- alone
- sometimes
- all night
- office
- carries
- bellhop
- dentist
- letter carrier
- taxi driver
- writer

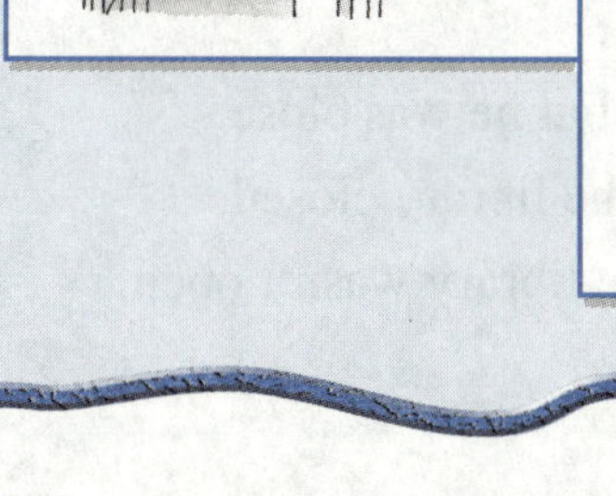

Test 2

Listen to four of the people above talk about work and write the number of each person on the correct picture.

LISTENING COMPREHENSION EXERCISES

Choose the best answer to each question.

1. (A) The prices are reasonable.
(B) The store is too far out of town.
(C) He would like the woman to repeat what she said.
(D) He agrees with the woman.

2. (A) It's rained unusually hard this year.
(B) There hasn't been any rain for many years.
(C) It's been many years since it rained.
(D) He doesn't like rain.

3. (A) He needs to do a better job writing questions.
(B) He certainly must make his writing better.
(C) Without the questions, he cannot write the answers.
(D) He needs to understand the written questions better.

4. (A) The agent was standing in line with his passport.
(B) The line to get new passports is very long.
(C) The woman must wait her turn to get her passport checked.
(D) He can check her passport instead of the agent.

5. (A) He couldn't finish closing the library book.
(B) He hadn't finished the library assignment, but he was close.
(C) He was working on the assignment when the library closed.
(D) His homework was incomplete because the library wasn't open.

Unit 6 Transportation

Warm-up: Pre-listening Exercises

Listen to the mini-dialogues two times each looking at the pictures below. You can write or make notes of the mini-dialogues in the margin.

A. I'm waiting for a bus.

B. The transportation system is terribly overcrowded.

Background for Listening Practice

A. ***Read the following paragraph with a low voice while listening to the tape.***

Modern transportation seems to be getting faster and faster. Not many years ago a trip around the world was long and dangerous. Today a jet plane can circle the globe in a few hours. Even travel to the moon is possible. But actually there are many problems still unsolved in the transportation systems of most ordinary cities.

Take Seoul, for instance. Although its transportation system is considered to be one of the best in the world, it is terribly overcrowded. During rush hour, for example, it is almost impossible to get on city buses and subway trains. Before we worry about traveling to the moon, we should improve the transportation systems of our cities and towns.

B. ***Study the following words and then fill in the blanks with the correct words.***

transportation	transferring or conveying from one place to another
circle	to enclose in or to move around
globe	something spherical or rounded, a spherical representation of the earth
overcrowded	to cause to be too crowded, to crowd together too much
improve	to advance or make progress in what is desirable

1. How long does a jet plane circle the ______ in an hour?
2. Seoul is terribly ______ compared to other cities.
3. If you practice English conversation continuously, your English proficiency will be ______ soon.
4. How many times does the earth ______ the sun in a year?
5. Modern ______ will be getting faster.

C. ***Listen to the tape again.***

Oral Practice & Writing Exercises

A.* *Now let's practice. Please repeat, considering the paragraph in the "Background for Listening Practice".

1. Modern transportation seems to be getting fast.
2. Today a jet plane can circle the globe in a few hours.
3. Even travel to the moon is possible.
4. There are many problems still unsolved in the transportation system.
5. It is almost impossible to get on city buses.

B.* *Change the present verb into the past verb.

1. long ➡ ______	2. dangerous ➡ ______
3. possible ➡ ______	4. actual ➡ ______
5. ordinary ➡ ______	6. terrible ➡ ______

C.* *Now dictate the following sentences while listening to them once.

Modern transportation seems to be getting faster and faster. Not many years ago a trip around the world was long and dangerous. Today a jet plane can circle ______ globe in a few ______. Even travel to the ______ is possible. But actually ______ are many problems still ______ in the transportation systems ______ most ordinary cities.

Take ______, for instance. Although its ______ system is considered to ______ one of the best ______ the world, it is ______ overcrowded. During rush hour, ______ example, it is almost ______ to get on city ______ and subway trains. Before ______ worry about traveling to ______ moon, we should improve ______ transportation systems of our ______ and towns.

D.* *Listen again and check the answers.

Model Dialogue

A. ***Listen to the dialogue.***

A: Excuse me. I'm late for a meeting.
Can you tell me which bus goes downtown?

B: Sure. It's number twelve, but it just left and won't come again for an hour.

A: Oh, that's too long! I'll try the subway.
Does it go straight to downtown from here?

B: No, it doesn't. You'll have to transfer to the number three line.

A: That sounds like it will take long.
How else can I get to downtown from here?

B: Well, you can take a taxi.

B. ***Repeat the dialogue above.***

C. ***Now dictate the following sentences while listening to them once.***

1. Can you tell me ______ goes downtown?
2. But it just ______ and won't come again for ______ hour.
3. You'll have to ______ to the number three line.
4. That ______ like it will take ______.
5. How ______ can I get to ______ from here?

D. ***Listen again and check the answers.***

Pair Work: Interactions

Practice the following dialogue with your partner. Student 1 takes part A and student 2 takes part B. Then switch.

***A*:** Excuse me. I'm late for a meeting. Can you tell me which bus goes downtown?

***B*:** Sure. It's number twelve, but it just left and won't come again for an hour.

***A*:** Oh, that's too long! I'll try the subway. Does it go straight to downtown from here?

***B*:** No, it doesn't. You'll have to transfer to the number three line.

***A*:** That sounds like it will take long. How else can I get to downtown from here?

***B*:** Well, you can take a taxi.

Listening Comprhension Check-up

Listen to the paragraph again and write your answers in the space provided below. The instructor asks each question two times.

1. Does modern transportation seem to be getting faster?

2. Is travel to the moon possible?

3. Are there many problems still unsolved in the transportation system now?

4. Is it almost impossible to get on city buses and subway trains during rush hour in Seoul?

5. Is Seoul terribly overcrowded?

Can you summarize the paragraph 'Transportation' above in less than twenty words?

LISTENING TEST

Test 1

Listen to the conversation between Amy and Betty. Amy is talking about her cat, Asia, and Betty is talking about her two cats, Bebe and Bell. And then, number the pictures from 1 to 12 as you listen.

Test 2

Listen again and write the action below each picture.

Test 3

Listen and circle true or false for each sentence.

1. True False
2. True False
3. True False
4. True False
5. True False
6. True False
7. True False
8. True False
9. True False
10. True False

LISTENING COMPREHENSION EXERCISES

Choose the best answer to each question.

1. (A) All the lawyer's preparation did no good.
(B) The lawyer prepared nothing for the case.
(C) It wasn't work for the lawyer to prepare for the case.
(D) The lawyer didn't work to prepare for the case.

2. (A) The history class begins next week.
(B) He thinks the papers should be turned in next week.
(C) He has already done the paper for next week.
(D) The papers are not due next week.

3. (A) He's not really happy.
(B) The contractor's work was satisfactory.
(C) He would rather work with the contractor himself.
(D) He was already contacted about the work.

4. (A) The man should try another type of paper.
(B) The man should locate a typist tomorrow morning.
(C) The man should make a tape in the morning.
(D) The man should complete the paper without help.

5. (A) She'd like some pie.
(B) It's easy to buy it.
(C) The task the man's working on isn't difficult.
(D) It's easier to prepare pie than do what the man is doing.

Unit 7 Young People in America

Warm-up: Pre-listening Exercises

Listen to the mini-dialogues two times each looking at the pictures below. You can write or make notes of the mini-dialogues in the margin.

A. When's the Wedding?

B. I took care of my mother-in-law for four days.

Background for Listening Practice

A. ***Read the following paragraph with a low voice while listening to the tape.***

In America boys and girls start dating in their teens. They can meet their future mates in many different ways. Sometimes they are introduced by a friend, and sometimes they meet each other in school, at a party, or at work. The average age of marriage for women in America is 20-21, and for men 22-23. Before a couple gets married, they usually get engaged and the man gives the woman an engagement ring.

B. ***Study the following words and then fill in the blanks with the correct words.***

mate	a friend, someone's wife, husband or sexual partner
average	a single value that summarizes or represents the general significant
marriage	the relationship between a husband and a wife, the act of marrying someone
couple	two people who are married, living together
engage	to bind to do something, to bind by a pledge to marry
engagement ring	a ring worn by a woman when she is engaged to be married

1. The ________ adult man burns 1,500 to 2,000 calories per day.
2. In twenty years of ________ he has only taken two proper vacation.
3. As the four ________ began the opening dance, they were an odd couple.
4. He has found his ideal ________.
5. Her ________ is very expensive and bright.
6. Before a couple get married, they usually get ________.

C. ***Listen to the tape again.***

Oral Practice & Writing Exercises

A. ***Now let's practice. Please repeat, considering the paragraph in the "Background for Listening Practice".***

1. In America boys and girls start dating in their teens.
2. They can meet their future mates in many different ways.
3. Sometimes they are introduced by a friend.
4. The average age of marriage for women is twenty to twenty-one.
5. Before a couple gets married, the man gives the woman an engagement ring.

B. ***Write five nouns and five verbs which you heard in the paragraph.***

Nouns	Verbs
1. ______	1. ______
2. ______	2. ______
3. ______	3. ______
4. ______	4. ______
5. ______	5. ______

C. ***Now dictate the following sentences while listening to them once.***

In America boys and girls start dating in their teens. They can meet ______ future mates in ______ different ways. Sometimes ______ are introduced by ______ friend, and sometimes ______ meet each other ______ school, at a ______, or at work. ______ average age of ______ for women in ______ is 20-21, and ______ men 22-23. Before ______ couple gets married, ______ usually get engaged ______ the man gives ______ woman an engagement ______.

D. ***Listen again and check the answers.***

Model Dialogue

A. **Listen to the dialogue.**

***A*:** What kind of wedding do you want to have, Diane? A big one or a small one?

***B*:** A big one! I want all my friends and family to be there. How about you, Maria?

***A*:** I want a small one. Just my mom, dad and a few close friends.

***B*:** The bigger the better I think. I want to get married in a big church, too.

***A*:** Not me. I'm going to get married at City Hall.

***B*:** That sounds boring.

***A*:** I don't care. I just want to save money.

***B*:** But aren't your mom and dad going to pay for it?

***A*:** No, Diane. My parents aren't rich like yours.

B. **Repeat the dialogue above.**

C. **Now dictate the following sentences while listening to them once.**

1. What kind of ________ do you want to have?
2. I want ________ my friends and family to ________ there.
3. I want to get ________ in a big church.
4. I'm going to ________ married at City Hall.
5. But aren't your ________ and dad going to ________ for it?

D. **Listen again and check the answers.**

Pair Work: Interactions

Practice the following dialogue with your partner. Student 1 takes part A and student 2 takes part B. Then switch.

***A*:** What kind of wedding do you want to have, Diane? A big one or a small one?

***B*:** A big one! I want all my friends and family to be there. How about you, Maria?

***A*:** I want a small one. Just my mom, dad and a few close friends.

***B*:** The bigger the better I think. I want to get married in a big church, too.

***A*:** Not me. I'm going to get married at City Hall.

***B*:** That sounds boring.

***A*:** I don't care. I just want to save money.

***B*:** But aren't your mom and dad going to pay for it?

***A*:** No, Diane. My parents aren't rich like yours.

Listening Comprhension Check-up

Listen to the paragraph again and write your answers in the space provided below. The instructor asks each question two times.

1. When do boys and girls start dating in America?
2. When do American women usually marry?
3. What does the man usually give the woman when they get married?
4. When do American men usually marry?
5. Are boys and girls sometimes introduced by their parents?

Can you summarize the paragraph 'Young People in America' above in less than twenty words?

LISTENING TEST

Test 1

Listen to the conversation 1~5 and write the number of each conversation on the correct picture.

Test 2

Listen again and write the key words next to each picture.

LISTENING COMPREHENSION EXERCISES

Choose the best answer to each question.

1. (A) He reported that time for the budget meeting had been set.
(B) He is always late in submitting his accounting figures.
(C) He never manages to budget his time well.
(D) He is never too late in turning in his reports.

2. (A) The repairs that the mechanic had indicated were already made.
(B) The car is going to need a lot of repairs.
(C) Buying a new car would be quite expensive.
(D) The mechanic extended the repair warranty.

3. (A) Betty wrote the letter as directed.
(B) The directions were given to Betty in a letter.
(C) Betty will follow the instructions later.
(D) Betty worked exactly as instructed.

4. (A) Walter's had a lack of success with his business.
(B) Walter's failed in business.
(C) Walter's new company is doing rather well.
(D) Walter hoped to succeed in business.

5. (A) He should put the organ in the closet.
(B) The closet has already been organized.
(C) He needs to rearrange the closet.
(D) He wishes the closet were closer.

Unit 8 Birthdays in America

Warm-up: Pre-listening Exercises

Listen to the mini-dialogues two times each looking at the pictures below. You can write or make notes of the mini-dialogues in the margin.

A. My mother told me to invite you.

B. Do you have any plans for your birthday?

Background for Listening Practice

A. ***Read the following paragraph with a low voice while listening to the tape.***

Birthday celebrations are very popular among American children. The birthday child's mother usually invites his or her friends. They bring toys, books and other gifts. The mother makes a delicious cake and buys some ice cream and soda.

The mother carries the birthday cake into the room. It has many lit candles on it. Everyone sings "Happy Birthday" to the birthday child. Then he or she has to blow out all the candles. He or she always blows hard. The mother cuts the cake into many pieces. The children eat cake and ice cream and drink lots of soda. After that, they sometimes play games. Soon, it is time to go home.

B. ***Study the following words and then fill in the blanks with the correct words.***

celebration	noun of verb 'celebrate'; to 'perform publicly, to honor by solemn ceremonies', a special enjoyable event
gift	something that you give someone as a present
delicious	affording great pleasure, appealing to one of the bodily senses of taste or smell
carry	to move while supporting
lit	past participle of verb 'light'
blow out	to move or be carried by or as if by wind

1. He ________ the plate through to the dinning room.
2. Food that is ________ has a very pleasant taste.
3. How many ________ candles do you need when you are ten years old?
4. For the party, there was a ________ in our house last night.
5. They believed the unborn child was a ________ from God.
6. If you ________ a flame or a candle, you blow at it so that it stops burning.

C. ***Listen to the tape again.***

Oral Practice & Writing Exercises

A. Now let's practice. Please repeat, considering the paragraph in the "Background for Listening Practice".

1. Birthday celebrations are very popular among American children.
2. They bring toys, books and other gifts.
3. The mother carries the birthday cake into the room.
4. He or she has to blow out all the candles.
5. The mother cuts the cake into many pieces.

B. Write five nouns and five verbs which you heard in the paragraph.

Adjectives	Nouns
1. ____	1. ____
2. ____	2. ____
3. ____	3. ____
4. ____	4. ____
5. ____	5. ____

C. Now dictate the following sentences while listening to them once.

Birthday celebrations are very popular among American children. The birthday child's ____ usually invites his ____. They bring toys, ____ and other gifts. ____ mother makes a ____ cake and buys ____ ice cream and ____.

The mother carries ____ birthday cake into ____ room. It has ____ lit candles on ____. Everyone sings "Happy ____" to the birthday ____. Then he has ____ blow out all ____ candles. He always ____ hard. The mother ____ the cake into ____ pieces. The children ____ cake and ice ____ and drink lots ____ soda. After that, ____ sometimes play games. ____, it is time ____ go home.

D. Listen again and check the answers.

Model Dialogue

A. Listen to the dialogue.

***A*:** Happy birthday, Billy. I have a gift for you.

***B*:** What is it, Pablo?

***A*:** Open it and see.

***B*:** Wow! I've always wanted Rollerblades.

***A*:** Do you know how to skate with Rollerblades?

***B*:** No. Do you?

***A*:** I don't know how either.

***B*:** Let's not worry about that now. How about some birthday cake?

***A*:** Good idea!

B. Repeat the dialogue above.

C. Now dictate the following sentences while listening to them once.

1. I have ____________.
2. ____________ with Rollerblades?
3. I ____________.
4. Let's not worry ____________.
5. How about ____________?

D. Listen again and check the answers.

Pair Work: Interactions

Practice the following dialogue with your partner. Student 1 takes part A and student 2 takes part B. Then switch.

***A*:** Happy birthday, Billy. I have a gift for you.

***B*:** What is it, Pablo?

***A*:** Open it and see.

***B*:** Wow! I've always wanted Rollerblades.

***A*:** Do you know how to skate with Rollerblades?

***B*:** No. Do you?

***A*:** I don't know how either.

***B*:** Let's not worry about that now. How about some birthday cake?

***A*:** Good idea!

Listening Comprhension Check-up

Listen to the paragraph again and write your answers in the space provided below. The instructor asks each question two times.

1. Who usually invites the birthday child's friend?

2. What do the friends bring?

3. What does the birthday cake have on it?

4. What do the children eat and drink?

5. What does the mother bring into the room?

Can you summarize the paragraph 'Birthdays in America' above in less than twenty words?

LISTENING TEST

Test 1

Listen to the conversations 1~6 and write the number of each conversation on the correct picture.

Test 2

Listen again and write the key words next to each picture.

LISTENING COMPREHENSION EXERCISES

Choose the best answer to each question.

1. (A) The professor bought two books.
(B) The students had to purchase two books.
(C) The students sold two books to the professor.
(D) The students were required to read two books by the professor.

2. (A) The doctor returned to the office.
(B) Jim asked the doctor to come to the office.
(C) The doctor will not return until next week.
(D) Jim was told to come back.

3. (A) Go to work in the lab.
(B) Sample the work from the lab.
(C) Have the samples delivered.
(D) Send a note to the lab.

4. (A) Mary became the new class president.
(B) Sue took her place as class president.
(C) In place of Mary, Sue became senior class president.
(D) The senior class president replaced Sue and Mary.

5. (A) The panel was analyzed on the television program.
(B) A committee evaluated recent political events.
(C) The program featured a psychoanalyst.
(D) The panel discussed the television program.

Unit 9 A Cold Welcome

Warm-up: Pre-listening Exercises

Listen to the mini-dialogues two times each looking at the pictures below. You can write or make notes of the mini-dialogues in the margin.

A. Why are you looking at the clock?

B. We promised to meet here at midnight.

Background for Listening Practice

A. ***Read the following paragraph with a low voice while listening to the tape.***

On Wednesday evening, we went to the Town Hall. It was the last day of the year and a large crowd of people had gathered under the Town Hall clock. It would strike in twenty minutes' time. Fifteen minutes passed and then at five to twelve, the clock stopped. The big minute hand did not move. We waited and waited, but nothing happened. Suddenly someone shouted, "It's two minutes past twelve! The clock has stopped!" I looked at my watch. It was true. The big clock refused to welcome the New Year. At that moment, everybody began to laugh and sing.

B. ***Study the following words and then fill in the blanks with the correct words.***

Town Hall	a large building owned and used by the town council, city hall
crowd	a large group of people who have gathered together
gather	to bring together, to collect
strike	hitting one thing against another, hitting a clock to indicate time
shout	to utter a sudden loud cry or voice
refuse	to escape, to reject

1. The man signaled for me to ________ the children together.
2. You can also use the ________ to refer to the town council that uses this building.
3. A huge ________ gathered in a square outside the Kremlin walls.
4. When a clock ________, its bells make a sound to indicate what the time is.
5. If you ________, you say something very loudly, usually because you want people a long distance away to hear you.
6. He expects me to stay on here and I can hardly ________.

C. ***Listen to the tape again.***

Oral Practice & Writing Exercises

***A.* Now let's practice. Please repeat, considering the paragraph in the "Background for Listening Practice".**

1. It was the last day of the year.
2. A large crowd of people had gathered under the Town Hall clock.
3. The big minute hand did not move.
4. The big clock refused to welcome the New Year.
5. Everybody began to laugh and sing.

***B.* Write five nouns and five verbs which you heard in the paragraph.**

	Past Verbs		Nouns
1.		1.	
2.		2.	
3.		3.	
4.		4.	
5.		5.	

***C.* Now dictate the following sentences while listening to them once.**

On Wednesday evening, we _____ to the Town Hall. _____ was the last day _____ the year and a _____ crowd of people had _____ under the Town Hall _____. It would strike in _____ minutes' time. Fifteen minutes _____ and then at five _____ twelve, the clock stopped. _____ big minute hand did _____ move. We waited and _____, but nothing happened. Suddenly _____ shouted, "It's two minutes _____ twelve! The clock has _____!" I looked at my _____. It was true. The _____ clock refused to welcome _____ New Year. At that _____, everybody began to laugh _____ sing.

***D.* Listen again and check the answers.**

Model Dialogue

A. ***Listen to the dialogue.***

A: Happy New Year, Monica! It's almost midnight.

B: Oh, hi Carlos! I'm so excited to hear the big clock ring.

A: Me too! Any second now people will be singing and dancing.

B: Wait! Nothing's happening, Carlos. What time do you have?

A: Oh, no! It's two minutes past twelve. The clock has stopped.

B: What? We missed the New Year?

A: I guess so.

B: What do we do now?

A: Well, I guess we can start singing and dancing.

B. ***Repeat the dialogue above.***

C. ***Now dictate the following sentences while listening to them once.***

1. I'm so ________ to hear the big ________ ring.

2. Any second now ________ will be singing and ________.

3. It's ________.

4. What? ________?

5. I ________ we can start ________ and dancing.

D. ***Listen again and check the answers.***

Pair Work: Interactions

Practice the following dialogue with your partner. Student 1 takes part A and student 2 takes part B. Then switch.

A: Happy New Year, Monica! It's almost midnight.

B: Oh, hi Carlos! I'm so excited to hear the big clock ring.

A: Me too! Any second now people will be singing and dancing.

B: Wait! Nothing's happening, Carlos. What time do you have?

A: Oh, no! It's two minutes past twelve. The clock has stopped.

B: What? We missed the New Year?

A: I guess so.

B: What do we do now?

A: Well, I guess we can start singing and dancing.

Listening Comprhension Check-up

Listen to the paragraph again and write your answers in the space provided below. The instructor asks each question two times.

1. Where did we go on New Year's Eve?

2. In how many minutes would the Town Hall clock strike twelve?

3. When did people find that the clock stopped?

4. Did the big minute hand move or not?

5. What did the crowd do then?

Can you summarize the paragraph above in less than twenty words?

LISTENING TEST

Test 1

Listen to the conversation 1~4 and write the number of each conversation on the correct picture.

Test 2

Listen again and write the key words next to each picture.

LISTENING COMPREHENSION EXERCISES

Choose the best answer to each question.

1. (A) She didn't do the work.
(B) She gave the assignment her best effort.
(C) She finished the assignment even though it was difficult.
(D) She gave the man a signal.

2. (A) She said some terrible things.
(B) She didn't say anything nice.
(C) She didn't have any nice things.
(D) She said really wonderful things.

3. (A) New employees are rarely initiated into the company.
(B) New workers don't generally undertake actions on their own.
(C) New employees are initially rated.
(D) It's rare for employees to make new suggestions.

4. (A) The woman is more than a week late.
(B) The children would have wrecked the house later.
(C) The woman was so late that she was a wreck.
(D) He's glad that she was not any later.

5. (A) He had not gone to the store.
(B) He was still at the market.
(C) He was going to take care of the shopping.
(D) He always went to the market.

Unit 10 Do You Speak English?

Warm-up: Pre-listening Exercises

Listen to the mini-dialogues two times each looking at the pictures below. You can write or make notes of the mini-dialogues in the margin.

A. Could you drive me to the City Hall?

B. I live in a small village in the South of France.

Background for Listening Practice

***A.* Read the following paragraph with a low voice while listening to the tape.**

I had an amusing experience last year. After I had left a small village in the south of France, I drove on to the next town. On the way, a young man waved to me. I stopped and he asked me for a lift. As soon as he had got into the car, I said good morning to him in French and he replied in the same language. Apart from a few words, I do not know any French at all. Neither of us spoke during the journey. I had nearly reached the town when the young man suddenly said very slowly, "Do you speak English?" Just then I learned that he was English himself!

***B.* Study the following words and then fill in the blanks with the correct words.**

amusing	adjective of verb 'amuse', making you laugh or smile
wave	to motion with the hands or with something held in them in signal
lift	a free ride in a private vehiclel
reply	to answer; say or do as an answer
journey	travel or passage from one place to another

1. He ________ that this was absolutely impossible.
2. There is an express service from Paris which completes the ________ to Boad eaux in under 4 hours.
3. I gave him a ________ home yesterday.
4. Jessica caught sight of Lois and ________ to her.
5. He had a terrific sense of humor and could be very ________.

***C.* Listen to the tape again.**

Oral Practice & Writing Exercises

A. ***Now let's practice. Please repeat, considering the paragraph in the "Background for Listening Practice".***

1. I had an amusing experience last year.
2. On the way, a young man waved to me.
3. I stopped and he asked me for a lift.
4. I do not know any French at all.
5. Just then I learned that he was English himself.

B. ***Write a short sentence for each of the following.***

1. an amusing experience ➡ __________
2. as soon as ➡ __________
3. neither of us ➡ __________

C. ***Now dictate the following sentences while listening to them once.***

I had an amusing _____ last year. After I _____ left a small village _____ the south of France, _____ drove on to the _____ town. On the way, _____ young man waved to _____. I stopped and he _____ me for a lift. _____ soon as he had _____ into the car, I _____ good morning to him _____ French and he replied _____ the same language. Apart _____ a few words, I _____ not know any French _____ all. Neither of us _____ during the journey. I _____ nearly reached the town _____ the young man suddenly _____ very slowly, "Do you _____ English?" Just then I _____ that he was English himself!

D. ***Listen again and check the answers.***

Model Dialogue

***A.* Listen to the dialogue.**

***A*:** Excuse me. Do you speak English?

***B*:** Of course. I'm English.

***A*:** Oh, really? I thought you were French.

***B*:** That's funny. I thought you were French, too.

***A*:** No. I'm from England also.

***B*:** Is that so? Which part of England are you from?

***A*:** I'm from London. How about you?

***B*:** I'm from Wales.

***A*:** Well, it's a small world, isn't it?

***B*:** Absolutely!

***B.* Repeat the dialogue above.**

***C.* Now dictate the following sentences while listening to them once.**

1. That's funny. ______________.
2. Is that so? ______________?
3. ______________.
4. ______________, isn't it?
5. ______________!

***D.* Listen again and check the answers.**

Pair Work: Interactions

Practice the following dialogue with your partner. Student 1 takes part A and student 2 takes part B. Then switch.

***A*:** Excuse me. Do you speak English?

***B*:** Of course. I'm English.

***A*:** Oh, really? I thought you were French.

***B*:** That's funny. I thought you were French, too.

***A*:** No. I'm from England also.

***B*:** Is that so? Which part of England are you from?

***A*:** I'm from London. How about you?

***B*:** I'm from Wales.

***A*:** Well, it's a small world, isn't it?

***B*:** Absolutely!

Listening Comprhension Check-up

Listen to the paragraph again and write your answers in the space provided below. The instructor asks each question two times.

1. Did the speaker have an amusing experience?

2. Who waved to the speaker?

3. Did they greet each other in English or in French?

4. What did the young man say at the end of the journey?

5. Was he English himself or was he French?

Can you summarize the paragraph 'Do you speak English?' above in less than twenty words?

LISTENING TEST

Test 1

Listen to the conversations 1~6 and write the number of each conversation on the correct picture.

☐ **winter:** ____________

☐ **today:** ____________

☐ **open:** ____________
close: ____________

☐ **begin:** ____________
end: ____________

☐ **leave:** ____________
return: ____________

☐ **brother:** ____________
sister: ____________

Test 2

Listen again and write the key words next to each picture.

Example : "It's January the 26th." ➜____________

LISTENING COMPREHENSION EXERCISES

Choose the best answer to each question.

1. (A) In a department store.
(B) In a stationery store.
(C) At the post office.
(D) At the airport.

2. (A) The teacher gave the students a hand.
(B) The term papers were turned in.
(C) The students got the papers from the office.
(D) The teacher handed the papers to the students.

3. (A) The attendant checked the oil in Mark's car.
(B) Mark checked to see if he had enough oil in his car.
(C) Mark checked with the service station attendant.
(D) Mark wrote a check to pay for the oil.

4. (A) A delivery man.
(B) A famous chef.
(C) A clerk in a fast-food restaurant.
(D) An airline steward.

5. (A) They need new print for the additional copies.
(B) They can make extra copies if necessary.
(C) Printers are needed for the additional copies.
(D) Additional copies are needed immediately.

Unit 11 Sports

Warm-up: Pre-listening Exercises

Listen to the mini-dialogues two times each looking at the pictures below. You can write or make notes of the mini-dialogues in the margin.

A. Do you like sports?

B. Did you participate in Olympic Games held in Seoul?

Background for Listening Practice

***A.* Read the following paragraph with a low voice while listening to the tape.**

The athletes lined up on the field, each behind their flag. They were a fine-looking group. Bands played and choirs sang and people cheered. At that moment a young Italian boy came running into the stadium. The crowd roared. In his hand there was the Olympic torch. It had been carried in relays all the way from the sacred valley of Olympic in Greece where the games were first held many centuries ago. The crowd watched while the boy ran up the steps of a platform, held the torch high for a moment, and then lowered it into a marble basin. Flames leaped from the basin where the Olympic torch would burn throughout the games.

***B.* Study the following words and then fill in the blanks with the correct words.**

athlete	a person who is trained or skilled in exercises, sports, or games
choir	an organized company of singers, an organized group of persons
cheer	to applaud with shouts, to urge on or encourage by shouts
roar	to sing or shout with full force, to make a loud confused sound
torch	a burning stick of resinous wood
platform	raised horizontal flat surface, a raised flooring
marble basin	a bowl made by marble(limestone that is more or less crystallized)
flame	a hot bright stream of burning gas that comes from something that is burning

1. The heat from the __________ was so intensive that roads melted.
2. Muḥammed Ali was a great __________.
3. The audience __________ its approval.
4. He has been singing in his church __________ since he was six.
5. The athlete with Olympic torch stood in front of a __________.
6. A picture of the President was set on fire as the crowd __________ and sang.
7. Nick finished what he was saying and jumped down from the __________.
8. They lit a __________ and set fire to the chapel's thatch.

***C.* Listen to the tape again.**

Oral Practice & Writing Exercises

A. ***Now let's practice. Please repeat, considering the paragraph in the "Background for Listening Practice".***

1. The athletes lined up on the field.
2. Band played and choirs sang and people cheered.
3. In a young Italian boy's hand there was the Olympic torch.
4. It has been carried in relays all the way from the sacred valley of Olympic.
5. The crowd watched while the boy ran up the steps of a platform.

B. ***Write five nouns and five verbs which you heard in the paragraph.***

	Nouns		Verbs
1.		1.	
2.		2.	
3.		3.	
4.		4.	
5.		5.	

C. ***Now dictate the following sentences while listening to them once.***

The athletes lined up ______ the field, each behind ______ flag. They were a ______ group. Bands played and ______ sang and people cheered. ______ that moment a young ______ boy came running into ______ stadium. The crowd roared. ______ his hand there was the ______ torch. It had been ______ in relays all the ______ from the sacred valley ______ Olympic in Greece where ______ games were first held ______ centuries ago. The crowd ______ while the boy ran ______ the steps of a ______, held the torch high ______ a moment, and then ______ it into a marble ______. Flames leaped from the ______ where the Olympic torch ______ burn throughout the games.

D. ***Listen again and check the answers.***

Model Dialogue

***A.* Listen to the dialogue.**

***A*:** Okay, Jimmy. If you want to win the gold medal you'll have to work hard on your jumping.

***B*:** Right, coach. That's what I'm doing today.

***A*:** Remember, you have a lot of competition this year in the high jump event.

***B*:** I know. Especially the team from Kenya.

***A*:** So, you'll need a little luck, too.

***B*:** Well, I can't count on luck. So I'll just keep working on my jumping.

***A*:** That's the spirit! You know you can't count on luck.

***B*:** Then why did you say that?

***A*:** I was just checking your attitude.

***B.* Repeat the dialogue above.**

***C.* Now dictate the following sentences while listening to them once.**

1. ______________________ on your jumping.
2. That's ______________________.
3. You have ______________________ this year in the ______________.
4. ______________________ on my jumping.
5. I was just ______________________.

***D.* Listen again and check the answers.**

Pair Work: Interactions

Practice the following dialogue with your partner. Student 1 takes part A and student 2 takes part B. Then switch.

***A*:** Okay, Jimmy. If you want to win the gold medal you'll have to work hard on your jumping.

***B*:** Right, coach. That's what I'm doing today.

***A*:** Remember, you have a lot of competition this year in the high jump event.

***B*:** I know. Especially the team from Kenya.

***A*:** So, you'll need a little luck, too.

***B*:** Well, I can't count on luck. So I'll just keep working on my jumping.

***A*:** That's the spirit! You know you can't count on luck.

***B*:** Then why did you say that?

***A*:** I was just checking your attitude.

Listening Comprhension Check-up

Listen to the paragraph again and write your answers in the space provided below. The instructor asks each question two times.

1. Where did the athletes line up?

2. Who came running into the stadium?

3. What did a young Italian boy hold in his hand?

4. Who ran up the steps of a platform?

5. Who lowered the torch into a marble basin.

Can you summarize the paragraph 'Sports' above in less than twenty words?

LISTENING TEST

Test 1

Listen to the conversation and circle the things that Julie asks Larry to do.

Test 2

Listen again and check(∨) all the things that Larry agrees to do, and make an "×" on the things he can't do.

Test 3

Listen once more and make a note of why he can't do some things.

LISTENING COMPREHENSION EXERCISES

Choose the best answer to each question.

1. (A) She plans to talk a lot this month.
(B) She has a lot to say about the phone bill.
(C) The bill is high because she has a lot to say.
(D) She agrees with the man.

2. (A) Bill had never really been sick.
(B) Bill was too sick to come to class.
(C) Bill was sick of calculus class.
(D) Bill had forgotten about the calculus class that morning.

3. (A) The man should go out tonight.
(B) The man should stay home and relax.
(C) The man should work on the paper tonight.
(D) The man should go out Monday instead.

4. (A) The cafeteria was open in the morning.
(B) The cafeteria did not serve breakfast.
(C) The breakfast in the cafeteria was not very tasty.
(D) The woman never ate breakfast in the cafeteria.

5. (A) He believes that it is acceptable to park there.
(B) The parking lot is too far from their destination.
(C) He knows that they won't get a ticket.
(D) He knows where the parking lot is.

Unit 12 Thanksgiving Day

Warm-up: Pre-listening Exercises

Listen to the mini-dialogues two times each looking at the pictures below. You can write or make notes of the mini-dialogues in the margin.

A. Can we thank God?

B. I think God helped them.

Background for Listening Practice

A. ***Read the following paragraph with a low voice while listening to the tape.***

Thanksgiving Day was first celebrated in America by the Pilgrims in 1621. When their fields produced a rich harvest, the settlers invited Indians to share in a feast of giving thanks to God. Since that time, Americans have regularly had a festival of celebration after the bountiful harvest in the autumn. Today it is just as it was at the first Pilgrim feast. It is a day when families gather to give thanks for the year's blessings and good fortune.

B. ***Study the following words and then fill in the blanks with the correct words.***

Thanksgiving	the act of giving thanks, a prayer expressing gratitude
celebrate	to perform solemn ceremony publicly, to honor as a holiday
the Pilgrim	a group of English Puritans who sailed to North America in the Mayflower to escape from England and establish a new type of society where they could be free to practise their religion
harvest	the season for gathering in agricultural crops, to gather in a crop
settler	one that settles in a new region
feast	an elaborate meal often accompanied by a ceremony
bountiful	given or provided abundantly

1. Americans have regularly had a festival of celebration after the rich ________ .
2. We have had a ________ harvest.
3. Do you know a story of the ________ ?
4. Many people gathered to ________ a man who had a seventieth birthday.
5. Do you know when the ________ Day is celebrated in America?
6. The ________ invited Indians to share in a ________ of giving thanks to God.
7. If you reap the ________ , you benefit or suffer from the results of your past actions.

C. ***Listen to the tape again.***

Oral Practice & Writing Exercises

***A.* Now let's practice. Please repeat, considering the paragraph in the "Background for Listening Practice".**

1. Thanksgiving Day was first celebrated in America.
2. The settlers invited Indians to share in a feast.
3. Americans have regularly had a festival of celebration.
4. The festival of celebration was held after the bountiful harvest in autumn.

***B.* Write five nouns and five verbs which you heard in the paragraph.**

	Nouns		Verbs
1.		1.	
2.		2.	
3.		3.	
4.		4.	
5.		5.	

***C.* Now dictate the following sentences while listening to them once.**

Thanksgiving Day was first _____ in America by the _____ in 1621. When their _____ produced a rich harvest, _____ settlers invited Indians to _____ in a feast of _____ thanks to God. Since _____ time, Americans have regularly _____ a festival of celebration _____ the bountiful harvest in _____ autumn. Today it _____ just as it was _____ the first Pilgrim feast. _____ is a day when _____ gather to give thanks _____ the year's blessings and _____ fortune.

***D.* Listen again and check the answers.**

Model Dialogue

A. Listen to the dialogue.

A: Hi mom! It's been so long since I've seen you!

B: It's been too long, Sweetie. I miss you since you went away to college.

A: I miss you too, mom. But I'm not too far away.
Besides, I always see you on holidays like this.

B: I know, but I miss cooking for you. Are you getting enough to eat at college?

A: Of course, mom. But the cafeteria food is terrible compared to your cooking. By the way, what's for thanksgiving dinner?

B: Turkey, of course.

A: Great! I've always loved turkey on Thanksgiving Day.

B. Repeat the dialogue above.

C. Now dictate the following sentences while listening to them once.

1. It's been so ______ since I've ______ you!
2. Besides, ______ on holidays like this.
3. But I ______ cooking for you. Are you ______ enough to eat at college?
4. ______ compared to your cooking.
5. I've ______ loved turkey ______ Thanksgiving Day.

D. Listen again and check the answers.

Pair Work: Interactions

Practice the following dialogue with your partner. Student 1 takes part A and student 2 takes part B. Then switch.

***A*:** Hi mom! It's been so long since I've seen you!

***B*:** It's been too long, Sweetie. I miss you since you went away to college.

***A*:** I miss you too, mom. But I'm not too far away. Besides, I always see you on holidays like this.

***B*:** I know, but I miss cooking for you. Are you getting enough to eat at college?

***A*:** Of course, mom. But the cafeteria food is terrible compared to your cooking. By the way, what's for thanksgiving dinner?

***B*:** Turkey, of course.

***A*:** Great! I've always loved turkey on Thanksgiving Day.

Listening Comprhension Check-up

Listen to the paragraph again and write your answers in the space provided below. The instructor asks each question two times.

1. When was Thanksgiving Day celebrated first in America?
2. Did the settlers invite Indians to share in a feast?
3. Have Americans regularly had a festival of celebration?
4. When did Americans have a festival of celebration?
5. Who gathered to give thanks for the year's blessings?

Can you summarize the paragraph 'Thanksgiving Day' above in less than twenty words?

LISTENING TEST

Test 1 *What are the people buying? Listen to the three conversations and circle all the things that each shopper buys.*

Test 2 *Listen to each conversation again and write how many of each thing the shopper buys. Add up how much money each shopper spends.*

VOCABULARY

- toothbrush
- nailclipper
- aspirin
- Band-Aids
- baby powder

VOCABULARY

- pie
- French bread
- fruitcake
- cookies
- donuts

VOCABULARY

- camera battery
- lens cap
- film
- photo album

LISTENING COMPREHENSION EXERCISES

Choose the best answer to each question.

1. (A) In a photography studio.
(B) In a biology laboratory.
(C) In an office.
(D) In the library.

2. (A) He's a pilot.
(B) He's a flight attendant.
(C) He's a member of the grounds crew.
(D) He works clearing land.

3. (A) Wash the dishes immediately.
(B) Use as many dishes as possible.
(C) Wash the dishes for as long as possible.
(D) Wait until later to clean up.

4. (A) In a bank.
(B) In a restaurant.
(C) At a service station.
(D) In a beauty salon.

5. (A) A salesclerk in a shoe store.
(B) A shoe repairperson.
(C) A party caterer.
(D) A salesclerk in a fixtures department.

Unit 13 Chuseok

Warm-up: Pre-listening Exercises

Listen to the mini-dialogues two times each looking at the pictures below. You can write or make notes of the mini-dialogues in the margin.

A. Did your ancestors live there?

B. What did you do for Chuseok?

Background for Listening Practice

A. Read the following paragraph with a low voice while listening to the tape.

Chuseok is one of the biggest holidays in Korea. It is celebrated on the eighth full moon of the lunar year. The day before Chuseok, the buses and trains are packed with people traveling to their family's native place. At the same time, the country people are busy preparing delicious rice from the new harvest and special crescent-shaped rice cakes called Songpyeon.

Filial piety is the basis of traditional Korean culture and Chuseok is no exception. The most important part of the day is visiting one's ancestors' graves. The grass around the mound must be trimmed. Then the men line up before the grave and perform several deep bows. In this way, the memory of the elders is honored.

B. Study the following words and then fill in the blanks with the correct words.

lunar	relating to the moon
crescent-shaped	a curved shape that is wider in the middle than at its ends, like the shape of the moon during its first and last quarters
filial	relating to or befitting a son or daughter, describing the duties, relationships which exists
piety	strong religious belief, religious or dutiful behavior
mound	one constructed over a burial or ceremonial site, tomb
trim	to make grass neat, tidy, and attractive

1. Her ______ earned her a personal missive from Pop. Gregory VII.
2. His father would accuse him of neglecting his ______ duties.
3. Did you see the ______ moon yesterday?
4. Do Korean farmers refer the ______ calender when they engage in far ming?
5. Grass shears are specially made to ______ grass growing in awkward places.
6. The bulldozers piled up huge ______ of dirt.

C. Listen to the tape again.

Oral Practice & Writing Exercises

***A.* Now let's practice. Please repeat, considering the paragraph in the "Background for Listening Practice".**

1. Chuseok is one of the biggest holidays in Korea.
2. The buses and trains are packed with people.
3. The country people are busy preparing delicious rice from the new harvest.
4. Filial piety is the basis of traditional Korea culture.
5. The most important part of the day is visiting one's ancestors' graves.

***B.* Write five nouns and five verbs which you heard in the paragraph.**

	Nouns		Verbs
1.		1.	
2.		2.	
3.		3.	
4.		4.	
5.		5.	

***C.* Now dictate the following sentences while listening to them once.**

Chuseok is one of the biggest holidays in Korea. It is celebrated _____ the eighth full _____ of the lunar _____. The day before _____, the buses and _____ are packed with _____ traveling to their _____ native place. At _____ same time, the _____ people are busy _____ delicious rice from _____ new harvest and _____ crescent-shaped rice cakes _____ Songpyeon.

Filial piety is _____ basis of traditional _____ culture and Chuseok _____ no exception. The _____ important part of _____ day is visiting _____ ancestors' graves. The _____ around the mound _____ be trimmed. Then _____ men line up _____ the grave and _____ several deep bows. _____ this way, the _____ of the elders _____ honored.

***D.* Listen again and check the answers.**

Model Dialogue

A. Listen to the dialogue.

A: I heard that Chuseok is next weekend, Cheolsu. What kind of a day is it?
B: Oh, Chuseok is one of the biggest holidays in Korea. It's the harvest festival.
A: What do people do to celebrate?
B: Just about everyone goes to his family's native place.
A: Wow! The buses must be packed!
B: They are, and so are the trains.
A: Do you do anything special besides just meeting your family?
B: Well, I guess the most important thing is visiting our ancestors' graves.
A: Is there any special Chuseok food?
B: My favorite is the crescent-shaped rice cakes my grandmother makes.

B. Repeat the dialogue above.

C. Now dictate the following sentences while listening to them once.

1. Chuseok is ________________ in Korea.
2. Just about everyone goes to ________________.
3. Do you do anything special ________________?
4. Is there ________________?
5. ________________ my grandmother makes.

D. Listen again and check the answers.

Pair Work: Interactions

Practice the following dialogue with your partner. Student 1 takes part A and student 2 takes part B. Then switch.

***A*:** I heard that Chuseok is next weekend, Cheolsu. What kind of a day is it?

***B*:** Oh, Chuseok is one of the biggest holidays in Korea. It's the harvest festival.

***A*:** What do people do to celebrate?

***B*:** Just about everyone goes to his family's native place.

***A*:** Wow! The buses must be packed!

***B*:** They are, and so are the trains.

***A*:** Do you do anything special besides just meeting your family?

***B*:** Well, I guess the most important thing is visiting our ancestors' graves.

***A*:** Is there any special Chuseok food?

***B*:** My favorite is the crescent-shaped rice cakes my grandmother makes.

Listening Comprhension Check-up

Listen to the paragraph again and write your answers in the space provided below. The instructor asks each question two times.

1. What is one of the biggest holidays in Korea?

2. When is Chuseok celebrated?

3. Where do the men line up?

4. Why are the country people busy?

5. How is the memory of the elders honored?

Can you summarize the paragraph 'Chuseok' above in less than twenty words?

LISTENING TEST

Test 1

Listen to the conversation and write "A" on the things Adam did, and "B" on the things Brian did.

Test 2 ***Listen again and write what Adam or Brian did below each picture.***

Example : Adam → He went skiing.

LISTENING COMPREHENSION EXERCISES

Choose the best answer to each question.

1. (A) The man should spend more time on registration.
(B) The man should walk more quickly through registration.
(C) The man should send in his registration materials.
(D) The man should try to avoid registering next semester.

2. (A) He couldn't find Paula's phone number, so he didn't call her.
(B) He couldn't give Paula the list over the phone.
(C) When he went to call Paula, he couldn't find the list.
(D) He couldn't recollect the number that was on the list.

3. (A) She couldn't take her luggage to the store.
(B) She stored her luggage at the train station.
(C) She carried her luggage from the train station to the store.
(D) There were no lockers for her bags.

4. (A) The woman had taken a different major.
(B) The woman had chosen psychology as a major.
(C) The woman was uninformed.
(D) The woman needed to see a psychiatrist.

5. (A) She would like the man to repeat what he said.
(B) She thinks the exam could have been a little more difficult.
(C) She shares the same opinion of the exam as the man.
(D) She believes that the exam was easy.

Unit 14 Confucianism

Warm-up: Pre-listening Exercises

Listen to the mini-dialogues two times each looking at the pictures below. You can write or make notes of the mini-dialogues in the margin.

A. Do you know what Confucianism is?

B. Do you think Confucianism is a religion?

Background for Listening Practice

***A.* Read the following paragraph with a low voice while listening to the tape.**

Confucianism is concerned with the proper relationships between men. The five essential relationships are between king and subject, parent and child, husband and wife, elder brother and younger brother, and friend and friend. Humanity, justice, reverence and wisdom are emphasized. Above all, one must exemplify filial piety.

During the Yi dynasty, government officials were chosen by means of a civil service examination. Confucius' teaching was the main subject of the essay questions. In order to prepare students to pass this examination, private schools sprang up all over the country. The Chinese classics, especially Confucius' books, were studied thoroughly, one by one.

***B.* Study the following words and then fill in the blanks with the correct words.**

Confucianism	teachings of Chinese philosopher Confucius
essential	extremely important
humanity	state of being a human being, rather than an animal or an object
reverence	a feeling of great respect for someone
exemplify	to show or illustrate by example
spring up	suddenly appears or comes into existence

1. Here where it only rains every five or ten years, grass will ______ within days of a rainstorm.
2. ______ focuses on the proper relationships between men.
3. It was absolutely ______ to separate crops from the areas that animals used as pasture.
4. He was under discussion and it made him feel deprived of his ______.
5. We stand together now in mutual support and in ______ for the dead.
6. The room's style ______ Conran's ideal of beauty and practicality.

***C.* Listen to the tape again.**

Oral Practice & Writing Exercises

A. Now let's practice. Please repeat, considering the paragraph in the "Background for Listening Practice".

1. Confucianism is concerned with the proper relationships between men.
2. Humanity, justice, reverence and wisdom are emphasized.
3. One must exemplify filial piety.
4. Government officials were chosen by means of a civil service examination.
5. Private schools sprang up all over the country.

B. Write five verbs and five essential relationships which you heard in the paragraph.

	Verbs		Five Essential Relationships
1.		1.	
2.		2.	
3.		3.	
4.		4.	
5.		5.	

C. Now dictate the following sentences while listening to them once.

Confucianism is concerned ______ the proper relationships ______ men. The five ______ relationships are between ______ and subject, parent ______ child, husband and ______, elder brother and ______ brother, and friend ______ friend. Humanity, justice, ______ and wisdom are ______. Above all, one ______ exemplify filial piety.

During the Yi ______, government officials were ______ by means of ______ civil service examination. ______ teaching was the ______ subject of the ______ questions. In order ______ prepare students to ______ this examination, private ______ sprang up all ______ the country. The ______ classics, especially Confucius' ______, were studied thoroughly, ______ by one.

D. Listen again and check the answers.

Model Dialogue

A. ***Listen to the dialogue.***

A: Why won't you marry me?

B: Because you're the eldest son.

A: Don't you want to take care of my parents?

B: No, I don't. I just want to take care of our own children.

A: But a good wife should follow the customs of our culture.

B: And a good husband should consider what his wife wants.

A: You're making me crazy!

B: Sorry, but times are changing.

B. ***Repeat the dialogue above.***

C. ***Now dictate the following sentences while listening to them once.***

1. Because ______________.
2. I just want to ______________.
3. ______________ the customs of our culture.
4. A good husband ______________.
5. Sorry, ______________.

D. ***Listen again and check the answers.***

Pair Work: Interactions

Practice the following dialogue with your partner. Student 1 takes part A and student 2 takes part B. Then switch.

***A*:** Why won't you marry me?
***B*:** Because you're the eldest son.
***A*:** Don't you want to take care of my parents?
***B*:** No, I don't. I just want to take care of our own children.
***A*:** But a good wife should follow the customs of our culture.
***B*:** And a good husband should consider what his wife wants.
***A*:** You're making me crazy!
***B*:** Sorry, but times are changing.

Listening Comprhension Check-up

Listen to the paragraph again and write your answers in the space provided below. The instructor asks each question two times.

1. What is Confucianism?

2. What are the five essential relationships?

3. What does one have to exemplify?

4. How were government officials chosen during the Yi Dynasty?

5. What was Confucius' teaching?

Can you summarize the paragraph 'Confucianism' above in less than twenty words?

LISTENING TEST

Test 1

Listen to five conversations. In each of them, one person is asking another person not to smoke. Write the number of the conversation on the correct picture.

Test 2

Read each sentence. Then, listen and decide if the meaning is the same or different. Circle S or D.

S D **1.** You can smoke in my office.
S D **2.** I only want one.
S D **3.** This is the only place I can smoke.
S D **4.** We can put the windows in the car down.
S D **5.** Now you can't.
S D **6.** I can smoke here now.

LISTENING COMPREHENSION EXERCISES

Choose the best answer to each question.

1. (A) The service satisfied her.
(B) The food was worse than the service.
(C) She thought the service was bad.
(D) Neither the food nor the service was satisfying.

2. (A) He told his kids to leave.
(B) He seriously wanted the woman to go.
(C) He was joking when he told the woman to leave.
(D) He left with the woman.

3. (A) The project will take all their effort.
(B) They have no other work to do.
(C) It's impossible to finish.
(D) They aren't even close to finishing the project.

4. (A) She doesn't mind an hour more.
(B) She'd rather stay more than an hour.
(C) It's better to stay than go.
(D) She prefers to leave.

5. (A) The service at the hotel wasn't too good.
(B) This hotel gave excellent service.
(C) The service at the hotel could have been improved.
(D) This hotel's service was the same as the service at other hotels.

Unit 15 Christmas

Warm-up: Pre-listening Exercises

Listen to the mini-dialogues two times each looking at the pictures below. You can write or make notes of the mini-dialogues in the margin.

A. Do you believe in God?

B. What did you do on Christmas Eve?

Background for Listening Practice

A. ***Read the following paragraph with a low voice while listening to the tape.***

Christmas is the celebration of the birth of Jesus. It is traditionally held on December 25th. It is a time for generous gift giving, family reunion and general good feeling. Like other holidays, the joyous spirit of Christmas is often expressed by festive decorations and traditional food. On the front lawns of homes, trees and bushes are strung with twinkling electric lights. On almost every front door hangs some red and green symbol of the Christmas season: a wreath, a big red bow, or just the letters MERRY CHRISTMAS.

B. ***Study the following words and then fill in the blanks with the correct words.***

celebration	a special enjoyable event that people organize because something pleasant has happened
generous	giving more of something, especially money, than is usual or expected
reunion	a party attended by members of the same family, school, or other group who have not seen each other for a long time
spirit	the non-physical part of them that is believed to remain alive after their death
decoration	features that are added to something in order to make it look more attractive
wreath	an arrangement of flowers and leaves, usually in the shape of a circle, which put onto a grave or by a statue as a sign remembrance for the dead

1. German banks are more ______ in their lending.
2. The whole family was there for this big family ______.
3. I can tell you, there was a ______ in our house that night.
4. His ______ has left him and all that remains is the shell of his body.
5. The coffin lying before the altar was bare, except for a single ______ of white roses.
6. The only wall ______ are candles and a single mirror.

C. ***Listen to the tape again.***

Oral Practice & Writing Exercises

***A.* Now let's practice. Please repeat, considering the paragraph in the "Background for Listening Practice".**

1. Christmas is traditionally held on December 25th.
2. It is a time for generous gift giving, family reunion, and general good feeling.
3. The joyous spirit of Christmas is often expressed by festive decorations.
4. Tree and bushes are strung with twinkling electric lights.
5. On almost every front door hangs some red and green symbol of the Christmas season.

***B.* Write five adjectives and five verbs which you heard in the paragraph.**

	Adjectives		Verbs
1.		1.	
2.		2.	
3.		3.	
4.		4.	
5.		5.	

***C.* Now dictate the following sentences while listening to them once.**

Christmas is the ______ of the birth ______ Jesus. It is ______ held on December ______. It is a ______ for generous gift ______, family reunion and ______ good feeling. Like ______ holidays, the joyous ______ of Christmas is ______ expressed by festive ______ and traditional food. ______ the front lawns ______ homes, trees and ______ are strung with ______ electric lights. On ______ every front door ______ some red and ______ symbol of the ______ season: a wreath, a big red bow, ______ just the letters ______ CHRISTMAS.

***D.* Listen again and check the answers.**

Model Dialogue

A. ***Listen to the dialogue.***

A: Look, mommy! Daddy is bringing the Christmas tree into the living room.
B: Great! Why don't you go to get the decorations?
A: Okay. Can I put the star on top of the tree?
B: Of course, Honey. But let's save that for last.
A: Can I put the lights on them?
B: Sure. Let me help you.
A: Wow! The lights are blinking on and off.
B: Doesn't the tree smell good, Sweetie?
A: It sure does. Now can I put the star on top?

B. ***Repeat the dialogue above.***

C. ***Now dictate the following sentences while listening to them once.***

1. Why don't you go ______________?
2. ______________ on top of the tree?
3. ______________.
4. ______________, Sweetie?
5. Now can I put ______________?

D. ***Listen again and check the answers.***

Pair Work: Interactions

Practice the following dialogue with your partner. Student 1 takes part A and student 2 takes part B. Then switch.

***A*:** Look, mommy! Daddy is bringing the Christmas tree into the living room.

***B*:** Great! Why don't you go to get the decorations?

***A*:** Okay. Can I put the star on top of the tree?

***B*:** Of course, Honey. But let's save that for last.

***A*:** Can I put the lights on them?

***B*:** Sure. Let me help you.

***A*:** Wow! The lights are blinking on and off.

***B*:** Doesn't the tree smell good, Sweetie?

***A*:** It sure does. Now can I put the star on top?

Listening Comprhension Check-up

Listen to the paragraph again and write your answers in the space provided below. The instructor asks each question two times.

1. When is the celebration of the birth of Jesus held?

2. Is December 25th a time for gift giving, family reunion, and etc?

3. By what is the joyous spirit of Christmas expressed?

4. What are strung on the front lawns of homes with twinkling electric light?

5. What hangs on almost every front door?

Can you summarize the paragraph 'Christmas' above in less than twenty words?

LISTENING TEST

Test 1

Listen to these people talk about their jobs and write the number of the conversation on the correct picture. And then write one thing that the person likes about the job and one thing that the person doesn't like about the job in each blank.

He likes ________________.
He doesn't like ________________.

She likes ________________.
She doesn't like ________________.

He likes ________________.
He doesn't like ________________.

She likes ________________.
She doesn't like ________________.

Test 2 *Listen to each conversation again and write T or F.*

1. a) This person work and goes to school.
b) This person works the same time every week.

2. a) This person has medical benefits now.
b) This company gives medical benefits to all employees and their families.

3. a) This woman is the only female salesperson at this car dealer.
b) All of the men are friendly to her.

4. a) This person works alone.
b) This person works a lot of weekends.

LISTENING COMPREHENSION EXERCISES

Choose the best answer to each question.

1. (A) He would be glad to say it over again.
   (B) He would like the woman to repeat what she said.
   (C) He says that he would like to take the class again.
   (D) He's happy the class is over, too.

2. (A) He finished all the problems.
   (B) He doesn't believe what the woman said.
   (C) He was able to finish some of the problems.
   (D) Both he and the woman were unsuccessful on the math problems.

3. (A) The man had mailed the package.
   (B) The man had forgotten to go to the post office.
   (C) The man had given the package to the woman to mail.
   (D) The man remembered the package after he went to the post office.

4. (A) They should take both cars.
   (B) The woman should try not to be afraid.
   (C) The woman should buy a bigger car.
   (D) They should go together in his car.

5. (A) He want to know if the muffins taste good.
   (B) He thinks the muffins were recently prepared.
   (C) The muffins are not really fresh.
   (D) He's sure that the muffins were just made.

Unit 16 Always Young

Warm-up: Pre-listening Exercises

Listen to the mini-dialogues two times each looking at the pictures below. You can write or make notes of the mini-dialogues in the margin.

A. I want to be an actress.

B. How old does she look?

Background for Listening Practice

A. ***Read the following paragraph with a low voice while listening to the tape.***

My aunt Jennifer is an actress. She must be at least thirty-five years old. In spite of this, she often appears on the stage as a young girl. Jennifer will have to take part in a new play soon. This time, she will be a girl of seventeen. In the play, she must appear in a bright red dress and long black stockings. Last year in another play, she had to wear short socks and a bright, orange-coloured dress. If anyone ever asks her how old she is, she always answers, "My dear, it must be terrible to be grown up!"

B. ***Study the following words and then fill in the blanks with the correct words.***

actress	a woman who is an actor, a woman performing or acting on the stage or in the movies
in spite of	in defiance or contempt of, without being prevented by
stage	the part of a theatre on which the acting takes place and which often includes the wings
take part in	to have a share in an activity or event; participate in
terrible	exciting extreme alarm, formidable in nature

1. If you ________ an activity, you do it together with other people.
2. He was the first comedian I even saw on the ________.
3. If you feel ________, you feel extremely ill or unhappy.
4. She's not only a very great dramatic ________ but she's also very funny.
5. Josef Krips at the State Opera hired her ________ the fact that she had never sung on stage.

C. ***Listen to the tape again.***

Oral Practice & Writing Exercises

A. Now let's practice. Please repeat, considering the paragraph in the "Background for Listening Practice".

1. She must be at least thirty-five years old.
2. She often appears on the stage as a young girl.
3. Jennifer will have to take part in a new play soon.
4. She must appear in a bright red dress.
5. She had to wear short socks and a bright, orange-coloured dress.

B. Write five adjectives and five nouns which you heard in the paragraph.

	Adjectives		Nouns
1.		1.	
2.		2.	
3.		3.	
4.		4.	
5.		5.	

C. Now dictate the following sentences while listening to them once.

My aunt Jennifer is an actress. She must be _____ least thirty-five years _____. In spite of _____, she often appears _____ the stage as _____ young girl. Jennifer _____ have to take _____ in a new _____ soon. This time, _____ will be a _____ of seventeen. In _____ play, she must _____ in a bright _____ dress and long _____ stockings. Last year _____ another play, she _____ to wear short _____ and a bright, _____ dress. If anyone _____ asks her how _____ she is, she _____ answers, "My dear, _____ must be terrible _____ be grown up!"

D. Listen again and check the answers.

Model Dialogue

A. Listen to the dialogue.

A: Jennifer always looks so young.

B: How does she do it?

A: She eats healthy food and exercises a lot.

B: I'd like to do that, but I'm too lazy to exercise.

A: Me, too. Besides, I love junk food too much.

B: I guess we'll never look like Jennifer.

A: Well, we could start eating better and exercising more.

B: Good idea. What do you think about going to the gym?

A: Okay. But first let's have some ice cream.

B. Repeat the dialogue above.

C. Now dictate the following sentences while listening to them once.

1. Jennifer always ______________.
2. ______________ and exercises a lot.
3. And I love ______________.
4. We could ______________ and exercising more.
5. Let's ______________.

D. Listen again and check the answers.

Pair Work: Interactions

Practice the following dialogue with your partner. Student 1 takes part A and student 2 takes part B. Then switch.

***A*:** Jennifer always looks so young.
***B*:** How does she do it?
***A*:** She eats healthy food and exercises a lot.
***B*:** I'd like to do that, but I'm too lazy to exercise.
***A*:** Me, too. Besides, I love junk food too much.
***B*:** I guess we'll never look like Jennifer.
***A*:** Well, we could start eating better and exercising more.
***B*:** Good idea. What do you think about going to the gym?
***A*:** Okay. But first let's have some ice cream.

Listening Comprhension Check-up

Listen to the paragraph again and write your answers in the space provided below. The instructor asks each question two times.

1. Is the speaker's aunt Jennifer a nurse or an actress?

2. Does she often appear on the stage as a young girl?

3. What kind of dress will she wear this time?

4. What did she have to wear in another day?

5. Does she ever tell anyone how old she really is?

Can you summarize the paragraph 'Always Young' above in less than twenty words?

LISTENING TEST

Test 1

Darren just came home from shopping at the mall. He's talking to his wife, Julia. Listen to the conversation and number the things they talk about from 1 to 8 as you listen.

Test 2

Listen to the conversation again and check(∨) the things Darren bought.

LISTENING COMPREHENSION EXERCISES

Choose the best answer to each question.

1. (A) She is very busy.
(B) She has lots of free time.
(C) It is not necessary to take out the trash.
(D) She will do it if she has time.

2. (A) The interview is very important.
(B) He is worried about the interview.
(C) What he's wearing to the interview is important.
(D) He is not concerned about the interview.

3. (A) He has almost all the notes.
(B) His attendance was perfect.
(C) He went to all the lectures but one.
(D) He missed more than one psychology class.

4. (A) They passed the library at 6:00.
(B) The library opens at 6:00 in the summer.
(C) The library closes at 6:00.
(D) You can't check out more than six books in the summer.

5. (A) Water the plants once a day.
(B) Give the plants no more water.
(C) Water the plants often while the man is gone.
(D) Give the plants a limited amount of water.

Unit 17 Too Late

Warm-up: Pre-listening Exercises

Listen to the mini-dialogues two times each looking at the pictures below. You can write or make notes of the mini-dialogues in the margin.

A. Has your father ever arrested a thief?

B. Don't you want to be a doctor?

Background for Listening Practice

A. ***Read the following paragraph with a low voice while listening to the tape.***

The plane was late and detectives were waiting at the airport all morning. They were expecting a valuable parcel of diamonds from South Africa. A few hours earlier, someone had told the police that thieves would try to steal the diamonds. When the plane arrived, some of the detectives were waiting inside the main building while others were waiting on the airfield. Two men took the parcel off the plane and carried it into the Customs House. While two detectives were keeping guard at the door, two others opened the parcel. To their surprise, the precious parcel was full of stones and sand!

B. ***Study the following words and then fill in the blanks with the correct words.***

detective	one employed or engaged in detecting lawbreakers
valuable	adjective of noun 'value'; worth a good price, having desirable qualities
parcel	a wrapped bundle, package
thieves	pl. of 'thief', one that steals secretly
airfield	an area of land from which aircraft operate, airport
precious	of great value, high price, highly esteemed

1. A(n) ______ is smaller than an airport.
2. ______ objects and materials are worth a lot of money because they are rare.
3. He had a large brown paper ______ under his left arm.
4. The ______ snatched the camera.
5. Many of our teachers also have ______ academic links with Heidelberg University.
6. Now ______ are appealing to witnesses who may have seen anything suspicious last night.

C. ***Listen to the tape again.***

Oral Practice & Writing Exercises

***A.* Now let's practice. Please repeat, considering the paragraph in the "Background for Listening Practice".**

1. Detectives were waiting at the airport all morning.
2. They were expecting a valuable parcel of diamonds.
3. Someone had told the police that thieves would try to steal the diamonds.
4. Some of the detectives were waiting inside the main building.
5. The precious parcel was full of stones and sand!

***B.* Write five adjectives and five nouns which you heard in the paragraph.**

	Adjectives		Nouns
1.		1.	
2.		2.	
3.		3.	
4.		4.	
5.		5.	

***C.* Now dictate the following sentences while listening to them once.**

The plane was late ______ detectives were waiting at ______ airport all morning. They ______ expecting a valuable parcel ______ diamonds from South Africa. ______ few hours earlier, someone ______ told the police that ______ would try to steal ______ diamonds. When the plane arrived, ______ of the detectives were ______ inside the main building ______ others were waiting on ______ airfield. Two men took ______ parcel off the plane ______ carried it into the ______ House. While two detectives ______ keeping guard at the ______, two others opened the ______. To their surprise, the ______ parcel was full of ______ and sand!

***D.* Listen again and check the answers.**

Model Dialogue

A. Listen to the dialogue.

A: I've got bad news, captain. This box is full of nothing but stone and sand.
B: What? Where are the diamonds?
A: I don't know. Maybe someone switched boxes on the plane.
B: Who could have done that?
A: Well, the only suspects are the pilots.
B: Were there any passengers on the plane?
A: No. Only the pilots.
B: Ah-ha. Where are they now?
A: I've got worse news. They just took off.

B. Repeat the dialogue above.

C. Now dictate the following sentences while listening to them once.

1. ____________________, captain.
2. Maybe someone ____________________.
3. Were there ____________________ on the plane?
4. ____________________ news.
5. ____________________.

D. Listen again and check the answers.

Pair Work: Interactions

Practice the following dialogue with your partner. Student 1 takes part A and student 2 takes part B. Then switch.

***A*:** I've got bad news, captain. This box is full of nothing but stone and sand.

***B*:** What? Where are the diamonds?

***A*:** I don't know. Maybe someone switched boxes on the plane.

***B*:** Who could have done that?

***A*:** Well, the only suspects are the pilots.

***B*:** Were there any passengers on the plane?

***A*:** No. Only the pilots.

***B*:** Ah-ha. Where are they now?

***A*:** I've got worse news. They just took off.

Listening Comprhension Check-up

Listen to the paragraph again and write your answers in the space provided below. The instructor asks each question two times.

1. How long were detectives waiting at the airport?

2. What were they expecting from South Africa?

3. Who took the parcel off the plane?

4. Where were two detectives keeping guard?

5. What did the parcel contain?

Can you summarize the paragraph 'Too Late' above in less than twenty words?

LISTENING TEST

Test 1

Listen to the conversation 1~5 and write the number of each conversation on the correct picture.

Test 2 *Listen again and write the key words next to each picture.*

LISTENING COMPREHENSION EXERCISES

Choose the best answer to each question.

1. (A) He seemed to be rather hungry.
(B) She was quite angry at him.
(C) He was trying to hang the posters.
(D) She believes he was mad.

2. (A) The parents are going to stay up late.
(B) The parents have given Hannah her allowance.
(C) Lately, the parents have not been so loud.
(D) Hannah does not have to go to bed early.

3. (A) At a department store.
(B) At a service station.
(C) At a collection agency.
(D) In a delivery room.

4. (A) She just broke some eggs.
(B) They need to eat fast.
(C) She is serious about the boat.
(D) He has a choice to make.

5. (A) It was urgent that Ellen do her best.
(B) He really urged Ellen to do more.
(C) He was encouraged by Ellen to try harder.
(D) Ellen told him that she was trying to do better.

Unit 18 A New House

Warm-up: Pre-listening Exercises

Listen to the mini-dialogues two times each looking at the pictures below. You can write or make notes of the mini-dialogues in the margin.

A. Is your father a carpenter?

B. How many new houses have been built recently?

Background for Listening Practice

A. ***Read the following paragraph with a low voice while listening to the tape.***

I got a letter from my sister yesterday. She lives in Nigeria. In her letter, she said that she would come to England next year. If she comes, she will get a surprise. We are now living in a beautiful new house in the country. Work on it had begun before my sister left. The house was completed five months ago. In my letter, I told her that she could stay with us. The house has many large rooms and there is a lovely garden. It is a very modern house, so it looks strange to some people. It must be the only modern house in the district.

B. ***Study the following words and then fill in the blanks with the correct words.***

get a surprise	surprising, amazing
left	past of verb 'leave'
completed	past of verb 'complete'; finishing
lovely	lovable, delightful for beauty, harmony
garden	a plot of ground where fruits, flowers or vegetables are cultivated
district	a territorial division, an area, region

1. If you ________ something, you would finish doing, making, or producing it.
2. She ________ her degree in two years.
3. Varieties of these crops have been collected from all around the ________.
4. The beautiful ________ are open from 10:30 a.m until 5 p.m.
5. If she comes, she will ________.
6. It was just one of those ________ old English gardens.

C. ***Listen to the tape again.***

Oral Practice & Writing Exercises

A. ***Now let's practice. Please repeat, considering the paragraph in the "Background for Listening Practice".***

1. I got a letter from my sister yesterday.
2. If she comes, she will get a surprise.
3. We are living in a beautiful new house in the country.
4. The house has many large rooms and there is a lovely garden.
5. It must be the only modern house in the district.

B. ***Change the adjective into the adverb and write the antonym.***

Adverb		Antonym	
1. surprise ➡	____	1. Beautiful ➡	____
2. beautiful ➡	____	2. New ➡	____
3. complete ➡	____	3. Strange ➡	____

C. ***Now dictate the following sentences while listening to them once.***

I got a letter from my sister yesterday. She lives in Nigeria. ____ her letter, she said ____ she would come to ____ next year. If she ____ , she will get a ____ . We are now living ____ a beautiful new house ____ the country. Work on ____ had begun before my ____ left. The house was ____ five months ago. In ____ letter, I told her ____ she could stay with ____ . The house has many ____ rooms and there is ____ lovely garden. It is ____ very modern house, so ____ looks strange to some ____ . It must be the ____ modern house in the ____ .

D. ***Listen again and check the answers.***

Model Dialogue

A. *Listen to the dialogue.*

A: Welcome home Lizzie. What do you think of our new house?

B: I love it, Catherine. It's so much bigger than our old house.

A: Yeah. Now we have a garden, too.

B: Great! I want to see that, but first show me my new bedroom.

A: Of course. Get ready for a big surprise.

B: Wow! It's so big. And all my old books are here.

A: Look! Dad built you a new desk, too.

B: Oh! It's beautiful. It's so good to be home again.

B. *Repeat the dialogue above.*

C. *Now dictate the following sentences while listening to them once.*

1. What do you think ______________?
2. It's so much __________ than our __________ house.
3. But first show me __________ bedroom.
4. ______________.
5. It's so good ______________.

D. *Listen again and check the answers.*

Pair Work: Interactions

Practice the following dialogue with your partner. Student 1 takes part A and student 2 takes part B. Then switch.

A: Welcome home Lizzie. What do you think of our new house?

B: I love it, Catherine. It's so much bigger than our old house.

A: Yeah. Now we have a garden, too.

B: Great! I want to see that, but first show me my new bedroom.

A: Of course. Get ready for a big surprise.

B: Wow! It's so big. And all my old books are here.

A: Look! Dad built you a new desk, too.

B: Oh! It's beautiful. It's so good to be home again.

Listening Comprhension Check-up

Listen to the paragraph again and write your answers in the space provided below. The instructor asks each question two times.

1. Where does my sister live?

2. Where will she come next year?

3. When was the house completed?

4. Does the house have many large rooms?

5. What style does the house have?

Can you summarize the paragraph 'A New House' above in less than twenty words?

LISTENING TEST

Test 1

Listen to the conversation 1~6 and write the number of each conversation on the correct picture.

☐ **arrives:** ________

☐ **leaves:** ________

☐ **opens:** ________
closes: ________

☐ **breakfast:** ________
lunch: ________

☐ **starts:** ________
finishes: ________

☐ **opens:** ________
closes: ________

Test 2 ***Listen again and fill the time in each blank.***

Example: "It's twenty past ten." ➞ 10:20

LISTENING COMPREHENSION EXERCISES

Choose the best answer to each question.

1. (A) On a playground.
(B) In a parking lot.
(C) At a zoo.
(D) In a photo studio.

2. (A) Respond to the mail.
(B) Put the letters in a file.
(C) It depends on where the file is.
(D) File the answers she received to the letters.

3. (A) In an airplane.
(B) In a police car.
(C) In a theater.
(D) At a fireworks exhibit.

4. (A) Take care of Bob.
(B) Invite Bob to dinner.
(C) Let Bob know that they accept his invitation.
(D) Respond to the woman' s question.

5. (A) A pharmacist.
(B) A dentist.
(C) A teacher.
(D) A business manager.

Unit 19 Success Story

Warm-up: Pre-listening Exercises

Listen to the mini-dialogues two times each looking at the pictures below. You can write or make notes of the mini-dialogues in the margin.

A. Do you want to be a repairer?

B. I used to repair bikes and worked for fourteen hours a day.

Background for Listening Practice

A. ***Read the following paragraph with a low voice while listening to the tape.***

Yesterday afternoon Frank Hawkins was telling me about his experiences as a young man. Frank is now the head of a very large company, but as a boy he used to work in a small shop. It was his job to repair bicycles and at that time he used to work fourteen hours a day. He saved money for years and in 1938 he bought a small workshop of his own. During the war Frank used to make spare parts for aeroplanes. At that time he had two helpers. By the end of the war, the small workshop had become a large factory which employed seven hundred and twenty-eight people. Frank smiled when he remembered the difficult early years and the long road to success. He was still smiling when the door opened and his wife came in. She wanted him to repair their son's bicycle!

B. ***Study the following words and then fill in the blanks with the correct words.***

head	leader, director, president or one in charge of a department
company	a business organization that makes money by selling goods or services
repair	mending
workshop	a room or building which contains especially using wood or metal
spare	something that is not being used by anyone and is therefore available for someone to use
factory	a large building where machines are used to make large quantities of goods

1. There was hardly a ________ inch of space to be found.
2. He owned a furniture ________ in New York State.
3. Sheila found some work as a secretary in an insurance ________.
4. Many women know how to ________ their own cars in Japan.
5. ________ of government from more than 100 countries gather in Geneva tomorrow.
6. There are many modestly equipped ________ in America.

C. ***Listen to the tape again.***

Oral Practice & Writing Exercises

A. ***Now let's practice. Please repeat, considering the paragraph in the "Background for Listening Practice".***

1. Frank Hawkins was telling me about his experiences.
2. Frank is now the head of a very large company.
3. It was his job to repair bicycles.
4. During the was Frank used to make spare parts for planes.
5. Frank smiled when he remembered the difficult early years.

B. ***Write five adjectives and five verbs which you heard in the paragraph.***

	Adjectives		Verbs
1.		1.	
2.		2.	
3.		3.	
4.		4.	
5.		5.	

C. ***Now dictate the following sentences while listening to them once.***

Yesterday afternoon Frank Hawkins was telling me about his experiences as a young man. Frank is now the _____ of a very large _____, but as a _____ he used to work _____ a small shop. It _____ his job to repair _____ and at that time _____ used to work fourteen _____ a day. He saved _____ for years and in _____ he bought a small _____ of his own. During _____ war Frank used to _____ spare parts for aeroplanes. _____ that time he had _____ helpers. By the end _____ the war, the small _____ had become a large _____ which employed seven hundred _____ twenty-eight people. Frank _____ when he remembered the _____ early years and the _____ road to success. He _____ still smiling when the _____ opened and his wife _____ in. She wanted him to repair their son's bicycle!

D. ***Listen again and check the answers.***

Model Dialogue

A. *Listen to the dialogue.*

A: What are you doing?

B: I'm getting ready to deliver news papers.

A: How often do you do that?

B: Twice a day. At 6:00 a.m. and 9:00 p.m.

A: That's a lot of work, isn't it?

B: Sure it is. But some day I'll publish my own newspaper and I'll hire someone else to deliver them.

A: You're a dreamer!

B: No, I'm not. One day you will be reading my newspaper.

A: We'll see.

B. *Repeat the dialogue above.*

C. *Now dictate the following sentences while listening to them once.*

1. I'm getting ready ____________________.
2. ____________________________?
3. I'll publish ____________________.
4. ____________________ to deliver them.
5. One day ____________________ my newspaper.

D. *Listen again and check the answers.*

Pair Work: Interactions

Practice the following dialogue with your partner. Student 1 takes part A and student 2 takes part B. Then switch.

***A*:** What are you doing?

***B*:** I'm getting ready to deliver news papers.

***A*:** How often do you do that?

***B*:** Twice a day. At 6:00 a.m. and 9:00 p.m.

***A*:** That's a lot of work, isn't it?

***B*:** Sure it is. But some day I'll publish my own newspaper and I'll hire someone else to deliver them.

***A*:** You're a dreamer!

***B*:** No, I'm not. One day you will be reading my newspaper.

***A*:** We'll see.

Listening Comprhension Check-up

Listen to the paragraph again and write your answers in the space provided below. The instructor asks each question two times.

1. What was Frank Hawkins telling the speaker about?

2. When did he buy his won workshop?

3. What did he make during the war?

4. How many people did he employ?

5. What did his wife want him to repair?

Can you summarize the paragraph 'Success Story' above in less than twenty words?

LISTENING TEST

Test 1

Circle all the things that Zachary invites Mia to do.

Test 2 ***Listen again, and make an "×" on the invitation that she refuses, and check(∨) the one that she accepts.***

LISTENING COMPREHENSION EXERCISES

Choose the best answer to each question.

1. (A) He's sure about which chapters they are to read.
   (B) He thinks he knows what the assignment is.
   (C) He has to tell her how far she should go.
   (D) The professor told them to read the chapters after the exam.

2. (A) The man should take the pie out.
   (B) The man should try something else.
   (C) The man shouldn' t try cherry pie.
   (D) The man should feel sorry.

3. (A) He knows the movie starts at 8:00.
   (B) He is not quite sure when the movie begins.
   (C) He thinks the start of the movie has been changed.
   (D) He will start the movie himself at 8:00.

4. (A) Not doing the dishes now.
   (B) Leaving the house with the dishes.
   (C) Leaving later so that they can do the dishes now.
   (D) Washing the dishes before they leave.

5. (A) She's told Matt he'll go far.
   (B) Matt has far from enough talent.
   (C) She told Matt to roll farther.
   (D) She believes Matt has the ability for the part.

Unit 20 Percy Buttons

Warm-up: Pre-listening Exercises

Listen to the mini-dialogues two times each looking at the pictures below. You can write or make notes of the mini-dialogues in the margin.

A. Have you ever seen a beggar while in New York?

B. What do you think about beggars?

Background for Listening Practice

A. ***Read the following paragraph with a low voice while listening to the tape.***

I have just moved to a house on Bridge Street. Yesterday a beggar knocked at my door. He asked me for a meal and a glass of beer. In return for this the beggar stood on his head and sang songs. I gave him a meal. He ate the food and drank the beer. Then he put a piece of cheese in his pocket and went away. Later a neighbour told me about him. Everybody knows him. His name is Percy Buttons. He calls at every house on the street once a month and always asks for a meal and a glass of beer.

B. ***Study the following words and then fill in the blanks with the correct words.***

beggar	one that begs; a person who asks for food, money, gifts
knock at	strike something with a sharp blow, strike sharply
ask for	requesting, wanting
meal	the food you eat at breakfast time, lunch time, dinner time
neighbour	someone who lives near you
call at	visiting someone or something

1. The waiter offered him red wine or white wine with his ______.
2. One day I was surprised that a ______ midnight.
3. When I was on my way home, I saw that a beggar ______ every house on the street.
4. I decided to go to the next house and ______ food.
5. I began chatting with my ______ in the garden.
6. She went directly to Simon's apartment and ______ the door.

C. ***Listen to the tape again.***

Oral Practice & Writing Exercises

A.* *Now let's practice. Please repeat, considering the paragraph in the "Background for Listening Practice".

1. Yesterday a beggar knocked at my door.
2. In return for this the beggar stood on his head and sang songs.
3. He put a piece of cheese in his pocket and went away.
4. Later a neighbor told me about him.
5. He calls at every house on the street once a month.

B.* *Write five prepositions and five verbs which you heard in the paragraph.

Prepositions	Verbs
1. ______	1. ______
2. ______	2. ______
3. ______	3. ______
4. ______	4. ______
5. ______	5. ______

C.* *Now dictate the following sentences while listening to them once.

I have just moved to a house on Bridge Street. Yesterday a beggar ______ at my door. ______ asked me for ______ meal and a ______ of beer. In ______ for this the ______ stood on his ______ and sang songs. ______ gave him a ______. He ate the ______ and drank the ______. Then he put ______ piece of cheese ______ his pocket and ______ away. Later a ______ told me about ______. Everybody knows him. ______ name is Percy ______. He calls at ______ house on the ______ once a month and always asks for a meal and a glass of beer.

D.* *Listen again and check the answers.

Model Dialogue

A. ***Listen to the dialogue.***

A: Good morning, Mrs. Thompson. I sure am hungry and thirsty.

B: Oh, Percy! Not again. When are you going to get a job?

A: I have a job. I'm a singer and dancer.

B: I mean a real job. Like a cook or a janitor.

A: But I'm a great singer. Just listen to this new song.

B: Stop! I'll bring you a sandwich and a beer. Just don't sing!

A: Alright, Mrs. Thompson. Thank you.

B: You're welcome. And if you promise not to sing, I'll bring you another beer.

B. ***Repeat the dialogue above.***

C. ***Now dictate the following sentences while listening to them once.***

1. I sure am ______________.
2. When are you ______________?
3. I'm a great singer. ______________.
4. I'll bring you ______________.
5. If you promise not to sing, ______________.

D. ***Listen again and check the answers.***

Pair Work: Interactions

Practice the following dialogue with your partner. Student 1 takes part A and student 2 takes part B. Then switch.

***A*:** Good morning, Mrs. Thompson. I sure am hungry and thirsty.

***B*:** Oh, Percy! Not again. When are you going to get a job?

***A*:** I have a job. I'm a singer and dancer.

***B*:** I mean a real job. Like a cook or a janitor.

***A*:** But I'm a great singer. Just listen to this new song.

***B*:** Stop! I'll bring you a sandwich and a beer. Just don't sing!

***A*:** Alright, Mrs. Thompson. Thank you.

***B*:** You're welcome. And if you promise not to sing, I'll bring you another beer.

Listening Comprhension Check-up

Listen to the paragraph again and write your answers in the space provided below. The instructor asks each question two times.

1. Who knocked at the door yesterday?

2. Does the beggar call at every house once a week or once a month?

3. Who told the speaker about the beggar?

4. What is the beggar's name?

5. What did the beggar always ask for?

Can you summarize the paragraph 'Percy Buttons' above in less than twenty words?

LISTENING TEST

Test 1

Listen to the conversation 1~5 and check(V) the correct picture for each one.

1

2

3

4

5

Test 2

Listen again and write the number of each conversation(1 ~ 5) on any of the words that are used in comparisons.

long	delicious	nice	big
comfortable	handsome	cheap	roomy
sporty	good	mature	expensive

Test 3

Listen once more and complete each of the following sentences using one of the words from Test 2. Then compare sentences with a partner.

1. The white ones are __________.
2. The red one is __________.
3. The one on the right is __________.
4. The Phuket tour is __________.
5. The woman thinks hers is __________.

Listening Comprehension Exercises

Choose the best answer to each question.

1. (A) They should go to the hospital.
(B) Mary should visit the man.
(C) The woman should try not to break her leg.
(D) They should go on a trip with Mary.

2. (A) She knows where the children are.
(B) The children have finished playing ball.
(C) She's going to the park to find the children.
(D) She believes that the children are in the park.

3. (A) The man should try to borrow some from a neighbor.
(B) The man should take a check to Tom.
(C) The man should work on his math assignment with Tom.
(D) The man should check behind the door.

4. (A) He thinks the bill is due in the middle of the month.
(B) The bill is approximately fifteen dollars.
(C) He knows when they should pay the bill.
(D) The bill is going to be fifteen days late.

5. (A) They should postpone their decision until morning.
(B) They should go to sleep in the new house.
(C) They should not buy such a big house.
(D) They should decide where to go to sleep.

Unit 21 A Private Conversation

Warm-up: Pre-listening Exercises

Listen to the mini-dialogues two times each looking at the pictures below. You can write or make notes of the mini-dialogues in the margin.

A. Oh! That's a fantastic movie.

B. How many movies do you watch in a month?

Background for Listening Practice

A. ***Read the following paragraph with a low voice while listening to the tape.***

Last week I went to the theatre. I had a very good seat. The play was very interesting but I did not enjoy it because a young man and a young woman were sitting behind me and talking loudly. I got very angry. I could not hear the actors. I turned around and looked at the man and the woman angrily. They did not pay any attention. In the end, I could not bear it. I turned around again. "I can't hear a word!" I said angrily.

"It's none of your business," the young man said rudely. "This is a private conversation."

B. ***Study the following words and then fill in the blanks with the correct words.***

theatre	a building for dramatic performances or showing motion pictures
seat	a special chair of one in eminence, a chair or bench intended to be sat or. on
actor	one that acts; doer, one who represents a character in a dramatic production
attention	the actor state of attending through applying the mind to an object of sense or thought
bear	to hold in the mind
rudely	being in a rough or unfinished state

1. Ann could remember sitting in the back ______ of their car.
2. You have to be a very good ______ to play that part.
3. Each year more than two million household in juries need medical ______.
4. I could not understand why she felt compelled to behave so ______ to a friend.
5. If a woman makes a decision to have a child alone, she should ______ that responsibility alone.
6. Very soon he took the first steps towards a career in the ______.

C. ***Listen to the tape again.***

Oral Practice & Writing Exercises

A.* *Now let's practice. Please repeat, considering the paragraph in the "Background for Listening Practice".

1. The play was very interesting.
2. A young man and a young woman were sitting behind me.
3. I looked at the man and the woman angrily.
4. In the end, I could not bear it.
5. It's none of your business.

B.* *Make short sentences using the following expressions.

1. last week ➡ ______
2. behind me ➡ ______
3. get angry ➡ ______
4. pay attention ➡ ______
5. in the end ➡ ______

C.* *Now dictate the following sentences while listening to them once.

Last week I went to the theatre. I had a very ______ seat. The play ______ very interesting but ______ did not enjoy ______ because a young ______ and a young ______ were sitting behind ______ and talking loudly. ______ got very angry. ______ could not hear ______ actors. I turned ______ and looked at ______ man and the ______ angrily. They did ______ pay any attention. ______ the end, I ______ not bear it. ______ turned around again. "______ can't hear a word!" ______ said angrily.

"It's ______ of your business," ______ young man said ______. "This is a ______ conversation."

D.* *Listen again and check the answers.

Model Dialogue

A. *Listen to the dialogue.*

A: Excuse me. Could you please be quiet?

B: I'm having a private conversation. It's none of your business.

A: But you're interfering with the play.

B: It's not against the law to talk in a theatre.

A: I'm warning you. Stop talking or I'll call the attendant.

C: Hey! Why don't you both shut up? I'm trying to watch the play.

A: Oops. He's bigger than us.

B: Right. We'd better be quiet.

B. *Repeat the dialogue above.*

C. *Now dictate the following sentences while listening to them once.*

1. Excuse me. ______________________?

2. But you're ______________________ the play.

3. It's not against the law ______________________.

4. I'm trying ______________________.

5. Right. ______________________.

D. *Listen again and check the answers.*

Pair Work: Interactions

Practice the following dialogue with your partner. Student 1 takes part A, student 2 takes part B and student 3 takes part C. Then switch.

A**:** Excuse me. Could you please be quiet?
B**:** I'm having a private conversation. It's none of your business.
A**:** But you're interfering with the play.
B**:** It's not against the law to talk in a theatre.
A**:** I'm warning you. Stop talking or I'll call the attendant.
C**:** Hey! Why don't you both shut up? I'm trying to watch the play.
A**:** Oops. He's bigger than us.
B**:** Right. We'd better be quiet.

Listening Comprhension Check-up

Listen to the paragraph again and write your answers in the space provided below. The instructor asks each question two times.

1. Where did the speaker go last week?

2. Who were sitting behind the speaker?

3. Could the speaker hear the actors or not?

4. Were they talking loudly or quietly?

5. What did the speaker say when he turned round again?

Can you summarize the paragraph 'A Private Conversation' above in less than twenty words?

LISTENING TEST

Test 1

Listen to the conversation 1~3 and write the number of each conversation on the correct picture.

Test 2 ***Listen again and write the answers to the questions.***

Conversation 1 What does she do? → ______.
Who does she work for? → ______.
Where does she work? → ______.

Conversation 2 What does she do? → ______.
What is she studying? → ______.
Where school does she go to? → ______.

Conversation 3 Where is she from? → ______.
Which part? → ______.
What does she do? → ______.

LISTENING COMPREHENSION EXERCISES

Choose the best answer to each question.

1. (A) The car stalled on the road.
(B) Someone took the car.
(C) Rob sold his car.
(D) Rob heard someone steal his car.

2. (A) Buying the bigger container.
(B) Putting the milk in the cart.
(C) Taking a carton that is smaller.
(D) Getting the milk tomorrow instead.

3. (A) The receptionist welcomed the businesspeople.
(B) The man created a shipping and receiving business.
(C) The businesspeople were rather greedy.
(D) The businesspeople greeted the receptionist.

4. (A) The police officer was stationed near the tourist.
(B) The tourist was forced to accompany the police officer.
(C) The tourist became mad at the police station.
(D) The tourist stated that the police officer never came.

5. (A) He hasn't seen her ideas.
(B) It was a terrible deal.
(C) He doesn't like the idea.
(D) It sounds magnificent to him.

Unit 22 Correspondence

Warm-up: Pre-listening Exercises

Listen to the mini-dialogues two times each looking at the pictures below. You can write or make notes of the mini-dialogues in the margin.

A. What did you see while in New York?

B. Where did you travel this time?

Background for Listening Practice

***A.* Read the following paragraph with a low voice while listening to the tape.**

I am very sorry I haven't written you since I left home six months ago, but it has been a busy semester for me. In spite of my heavy schedule, though, I have managed to have some fun.

Since my arrival in New York, I have gone on a tour of the city and visited some famous landmarks and tourist spots. I have taken some pictures to prove it, too. My roommates and I went to a football game and we have seen a few Broadway plays. I have eaten in many foreign restaurants and have already tried different international dishes.

***B.* Study the following words and then fill in the blanks with the correct words.**

landmark	an object(as a stone or tree) that marks the boundary of land
tourist	a person who is travelling for pleasure and interest
spot	a small area visibly different(as in color, material) from the surrounding area
prove	to test the truth, validity, or genuineness of
roommate	a person you share a rented room, apartment or house with
Broadway	the New York commercial theatre and an amusement world

1. We have been accused of exaggerating before, but unfortunately all our reports ________ to be true.
2. ________ is located in the area between the Avenue of the Americas and Ninth Avenue and from W 41st Street to W 53d Street.
3. I met your ________ and talked about a rented room.
4. Are there many famous landmarks and tourist ________ in this area?
5. The Ambassador Hotel is a Los Angeles ________.
6. Blackpool is the top ________ attraction in England.

***C.* Listen to the tape again.**

Oral Practice & Writing Exercises

A. Now let's practice. Please repeat, considering the paragraph in the "Background for Listening Practice".

1. I haven't written you since I left home six months ago.
2. It has been a busy semester for me.
3. I visited famous landmarks and tourist spots.
4. My roommates and I went to a football game.
5. I have already tried different international dishes.

B. Write five adjectives and five nouns which you heard in the paragraph.

Adjectives	Nouns
1.	1.
2.	2.
3.	3.
4.	4.
5.	5.

C. Now dictate the following sentences while listening to them once.

I am very sorry ______ haven't written you since ______ left home six months ______, but it has been ______ busy semester for me. ______ spite of my heavy ______, though, I have managed ______ have some fun.

Since ______ arrival in New York, ______ have gone on a ______ of the city and ______ some famous landmarks and ______ spots. I have taken ______ pictures to prove it, ______. My roommates and I ______ to a football game ______ we have seen a ______ Broadway plays. I have eaten in many foreign restaurants and have already tried different international dishes.

D. Listen again and check the answers.

Model Dialogue

A. ***Listen to the dialogue.***

A: Let's go to Central Park today.

B: Okay. Let's take a taxi.

A: I've got a better idea. Let's take the subway.

B: Are you kidding? It's so dirty and dangerous.

A: I know, but taxis are too expensive.

B: Don't worry. I'll pay for it.

A: Really? Okay then.

B: There's just one thing.

A: What's that?

B: Can I borrow some money?

B. ***Repeat the dialogue above.***

C. ***Now dictate the following sentences while listening to them once.***

1. ______________.
2. It's ______________.
3. I know, but ______________.
4. Don't worry. ______________.
5. Can I ______________?

D. ***Listen again and check the answers.***

Pair Work: Interactions

Practice the following dialogue with your partner. Student 1 takes part A and student 2 takes part B. Then switch.

***A*:** Let's go to Central Park today.

***B*:** Okay. Let's take a taxi.

***A*:** I've got a better idea. Let's take the subway.

***B*:** Are you kidding? It's so dirty and dangerous.

***A*:** I know, but taxis are too expensive.

***B*:** Don't worry. I'll pay for it.

***A*:** Really? Okay then.

***B*:** There's just one thing.

***A*:** What's that?

***B*:** Can I borrow some money?

Listening Comprhension Check-up

Listen to the paragraph again and write your answers in the space provided below. The instructor asks each question two times.

1. When did the speaker leave home?

2. Was the first semester busy for him?

3. Where did the speaker visit?

4. With whom did he go to a football game?

5. What did he try in many foreign restaurants?

Can you summarize the paragraph 'Correspondence' above in less than twenty words?

LISTENING TEST

Test 1

Listen to the three conversations and write a number on each of the small pictures to show the order they are mentioned(1 ~ 11).

Test 2

Listen again and write an note about Bobby's plan below each picture.

Example : (1) buy a house

LISTENING COMPREHENSION EXERCISES

Choose the best answer to each question.

1. (A) Write a message to the man.
(B) Make some phone calls.
(C) Respond to the man's questions.
(D) Get a new phone installed.

2. (A) She's not sure if she's free.
(B) She's marked it on her calendar.
(C) She'll write a check for the calendar.
(D) Her calendar says she has to have a meeting at 3:00.

3. (A) He barely rode the bicycle.
(B) He didn't have enough money.
(C) The bicycle didn't need to be paid for.
(D) He paid for the bicycle.

4. (A) She fixed the television.
(B) Bob made the television work.
(C) The woman looked at Bob on television.
(D) Bob works for the woman.

5. (A) He helped her say what she couldn't say.
(B) She was unable to say anything about him.
(C) He hasn't helped her very much.
(D) What he said was very helpful.